Natural Nutrition For Dogs

Revised Edition

About The Author

Debbie Daniel is certified in Natural Pet Care and has studied extensively in Canine Arthritis and Joint issues. Her approach is to educate pet parents on how to avoid many toxins in your pets lives along with keeping the joints healthy even into the senior years, and to help extend lives and reduce illness overall. Her mission is to help Pet Parents learn more on Holistic Integrative Remedies and Nutrition.

Copyright © Debbie Daniel
978-1978332942
Revised Edition October 23rd, 2017
All rights reserved.
No part of this book may be reproduced, scanned, or distributed in any printed or electronic form without permission.
Printed in the USA
Cover Designed by Debbie Daniel

I would like to acknowledge my 5 dogs Diamond, Stormy, Sydney, Callie and Carley that have taught me so much just from the many illnesses and joint problems along the way. My life changed when I adopted these girls. They are my life and every day I continue to learn from them. How they interact with one another, how they deal with pain and anxiety and when they need me the most. And most of all, bring me joy and make me laugh every day! These girls are work but it's worth it because they deserve a terrific life compared to the life they had before me. I owe it to them to make up for the past abuse they may have suffered throughout. And this is why I have learned to provide the best diet and protect them from our own environmental toxins in today's world.
RIP to Molly and Sassy!

Intro

This book is about making changes in your dog's life to help them to thrive in living a long healthy life instead of just surviving. Learning to feed a proper diet and reduce many illnesses and exposure to toxins. This is also great for newly rescued dogs that have come from the streets or animal shelters. As your dog ages, the joints start to wear, this book helps to eliminate or reduce arthritis drastically by incorporating certain things into your dog's life. Learning how to prevent and treat heartworms using all-natural methods, supplemental treatment and diet for cancer, treating heart disease with home remedies, anxieties/fears and dealing with allergies.

This book will give you lots of information and precautions with certain supplements and disease, detailed dosing amounts and how to make the best decision for your dog's health and longevity. It is a great reference to revert back to when in need of answers for any arising issues.

Our recommendations and solutions using holistic and natural health care, nutrition and herbal remedies.

Remember: *Always know what's ahead instead of waiting for what's to come. Prevention has always been the best medicine.*

Contents

Ch. 1-Kibble And Pet Foods..................................4

Ch. 2-Allergic Reactions In Pets..........................10

Ch. 3-Homemade Diets for Dogs.........................19

Ch. 4-Supplementation......................................61

Ch. 5-Canine Arthritis & Join Pain.....................81

Ch. 6-Flea and Tick Medications.......................115

Ch. 7-Heartworm Treatment/Prevention...........120

Ch. 8-Heart Disease...128

Ch. 9-Storm Anxiety..138

Ch. 10- Cancer-Prevention, Treatment and Diet....144

Ch. 11-Healing Herbs......................................188

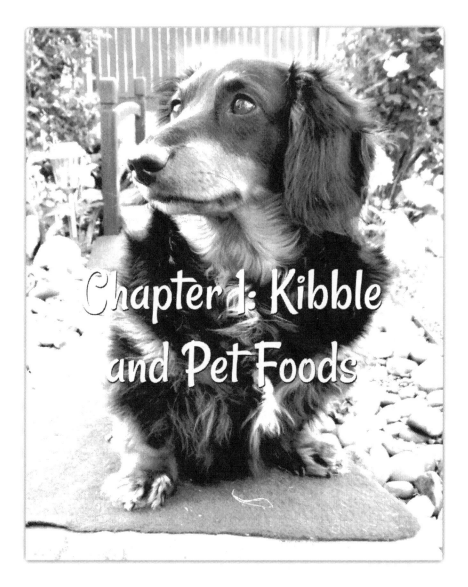

Chapter 1: Kibble and Pet Foods

Chapter 1
Kibble and Pet Foods

Carnivores cannot digest properly when eating foods like corn, wheat, rice or potatoes without stressing out the digestive system – and yet these are the ingredients in the majority of pet foods that the manufacturers use as primary ingredients in their formulas. Fortunately, most dogs are tough. Not only do they not die immediately eating inappropriate foods, but it often takes years before the significant physical destruction that occurs from a lifetime of eating the wrong foods before it becomes noticeable.

One of the reasons we're able to deceive ourselves into believing convenience pet foods are good for pets is because the changes to a pet's health and vitality brought on by a processed diet are usually not immediate or acute. The pet foods today have created dozens of generations of animals that suffer from degenerative diseases linked to nutritional deficiencies.

Many pet food companies use the cheapest ingredients they can find. Whether it comes from dead, diseased, road kill, or euthanized pets from shelters. These ingredients are not suitable for human consumption. If you won't eat it, why should your dog! Most pet foods contain 4-D ingredients. 4-D is meat and by-products that have been derived from animals that were rejected by food inspectors who classified the animals as not fit for human consumption because they were "Dead, Dying, Disabled or Diseased" at the time of inspection. Any chemicals that existed within that animal would still be inside of it when dead. Meat by-products are nothing more than slaughterhouse waste; waste that's been banned for use in human food and then sold to the pet food industry. It's what's left over after the slaughter and classified as inedible waste, unfit for human consumption.

With dry foods, the ingredients are cooked twice. First during rendering and again in the extruder. Altered proteins may contribute to food intolerances, food allergies, and inflammatory bowel disease.

High-heat processing of pet food creates potent carcinogens like acrylamide and heterocyclic amine. Needless to say, these cancer-causing by-products won't be listed on any pet food ingredient list. But they are extremely dangerous, even in small amounts, when fed day in and day out. There's a connection between these carcinogens and the rising rates of cancer in today's pets. Proteins, fats, antioxidants, enzymes, minerals, vitamins, and beneficial bacteria are all damaged or destroyed during the heating process. Grains and legumes contain mold and even through extrusion (400 degree temps), it does not remove or kill the mold. Mold can cause cancer and/or organ failure. Your dog has 10 times higher risk of getting cancer by feeding kibble foods than any other foods. Stay away from grains and fillers such as peas and potatoes. Also even though it isn't listed on the bag, pet foods are loaded with sugar. Nearly half of the bag is pure sugar although you won't find that on the label. The carbs break down into sugars. Do you really want to feed your dog this? Learn to read ingredients. Feeding these foods will shorten the life of your dog, because many horrible diseases like allergies, autoimmune disease, cancer, seizures, diabetes, arthritis/joint issues, gastrointestinal disorders, heart disease, kidney & liver failure, obesity, skin and coat disorders, and/or urinary tract disorders and you will be spending hard earned dollars on trying to save or care for your sick furry family member.

During extrusion this is what occurs;

- Starch gelatinization
- Inactivation of nutritionally active factors
- Protein denaturation
- Vitamin loss

Mycotoxin ("Myco" stands for "fungus") is still a big risk in dry pet foods even after the manufacturing process is complete. Before you start moistening your pet's food to try to replace the missing moisture, you should know about mycotoxins, another potential side effect of the use of grains in pet food. Mycotoxins are naturally occurring fungal by-products that can cause disease and death in pets. When grains are improperly stored, mycotoxins can develop. Two of the most common forms have been found in pet foods are aflatoxin and vomitoxin. Although mycotoxins are found all over the world they only become toxic in temperatures above 82 degrees and over 80 percent humidity at which point they interfere with cellular function, and are extremely carcinogenic and immuno-suppressive. Aflatoxin B1 is the most toxic of the aflatoxins and is the most potent liver carcinogen known.

We know that dogs and cats are carnivores, so why do we continue to feed these foods? Not only are the ingredients extremely questionable, pet food companies have no obligation to provide the details of the ingredients. In fact they go out of their way to try to change the names on contents to throw you off as well as leaving off vital information. Pet Food Companies will switch one preservative with some unpronounceable name for another. Even if the foods are processed here in the United States, doesn't mean it wasn't sourced from China. And if you ask them, they may tell you they are made and sourced in the USA, but that may not be true at all. And they can even change the source at anytime without notifying its buyers. Most all vitamins are sourced from China - even human vitamins, so it's best to buy from a reputable company. Do your research.

These large companies are hiding so much of the truth of what is truly in these foods; it's terrifying. Corn is a cheap filler ingredient, loaded with GMOs, non-nutritious for pets, and a known allergenic. Wheat is a big source of food allergies as well and can cause intestinal upset. Wheat is covered in Glyphosate (found in Round Up weed killer) as most all of our foods are coated in it. Soy (full of GMOs) is estrogenic and wreaks havoc on your pet's endocrine system. Even when people say they cannot digest gluten, it's more than likely not the gluten but the pesticides it's coated in. So many chemicals are causing our bodies to react and fight but when there are so many chemicals, your body just can't fight off the toxic effects day in and day out. I am certain dogs are going through the same thing on much higher levels.

Pet food companies are famous for using the **cheapest grains** they can find that are by-products of the human food waste industry. Why? How many recalls have we seen in the past several years? And it's apparent it will only get worse. Bags of dry pet foods have been filled with mold, rodents, worms, and moths to name a few. And how many bags have made humans sick from salmonella? Tons! And to top this off, studies found that the bag itself is leeching toxins into the foods.

Don't forget your 4-Ds:
4-Ds: Road kill, slaughter house rejects, animals that die on their way to meat packing plants - all are acceptable ingredients for pet food under the "4D" rule. Steroids, growth hormones and chemicals used to treat cattle including insecticide patches end up mixed into the final product.
Feeding kibble to your pet has almost always some irreversible damage. Kibble dehydrates the system leaving it lacking in moisture

which therefore causes kidney and bladder stones/crystals. Pets have to drink over 5 times the amount of water to stay hydrated throughout the day. Kibble also causes periodontal disease from buildup of chemicals, addicting additives and preservatives. Kibble is also loaded with sugar although you won't find that on the label. The bags are almost half sugar of the actual food in the bag. Unbelievable. Kibble almost always causes cancer and/or some form of kidney and liver failure as well as arthritis and food allergies. It may not occur immediately but over a period of time, it will take its toll on your pet. People think a dog living 10-15 years is great. It's not. Our pets should live double that time and they can if we change the diet and remove toxins, chemicals and the low quality ingredients in pet foods. When pets try to digest the kibble, the body has a very difficult time breaking down all the chemicals and additives, which overworks the entire digestive system causing other issues like vomiting, diarrhea, Irritable Bowel Syndrome (IBS), bloody stools, and colon cancer. To have a healthy gut, you must feed a species appropriate diet. This does not include feeding bagged, pouched or canned pet foods.

All pet foods (canned, bagged etc) including prescription diet foods recommended by your vet, are extremely deadly. Vets did not take a course in nutrition. Large pet food manufacturers like Purina and Hills come into clinics and give a 3-4 hour lecture of why these foods are much better than others and how they can help heal your pet. It's a ploy to sell more pet foods. Veterinarians do not know any better. And the ones that do are most likely your holistic veterinarians. Don't be totally trusting in your vet. He/She may not know how to read the ingredients and don't know what harm they can do. You, as a pet parent need to be vigilante and know what's best for your pets when it comes to diet, vaccines and medications. If you stand your ground, and still your vet will not accept the way you are feeding or your denial of vaccines, FIND A NEW VET THAT WILL! No one should tell you what you can and can't do on how to take better care of your pet. I only ask one thing, when changing the diet; please do your homework by researching, asking others, get in groups, and find the best balanced diet for your pet. I hope this book will help you a lot in answering those questions. It doesn't cost a fortune to feed a super good food to your pets. Even if you buy **expensive high quality kibble** (or canned), you're still buying junk and paying a fortune. Why pay for hamburger at a high price when you can buy steak for the same or lower price. Make a change today. You won't regret it! And remember, not only are these pet foods killing pets, so are the deadly tainted toxic treats. If you must buy treats, buy homemade from small mom and pop shops. Check ingredients. Search out organic ingredients.

DO NOT BUY grocery store or pet store treats!! There have been many deaths from these! As I always say, **"Better Safe Than Sorry".**

Stop buying these foods and supporting these companies or they will continue to sell them and more animals will die.

Most all of your gastrointestinal disorders are caused by diet and lack of nutrients and enzymes. Commercial pet foods are the hardest on the digestive system. Kibble takes a long time breaking down in the GI tract that puts the digestive system into an overly stressed situation and causing a slight dehydration at all times. Homemade is easier to digest and provides little to no stress on the digestive tract and provides extra moisture that is needed. It's time to make a change now so your dog can live a long healthy pain free life and this book will tell you how to do just that.

"Running to the store to buy a bag of pet food is nothing more than convenience to the human. But it is a slow death to your pet."

All disease begins in the gut. - Hippocrates

Throughout this book, I am going to sound like a broken record. It is so that you will understand the importance of what I am saying and how it applies to every ailment or daily activity. And I hope it will come naturally to you by the time you finish so that you won't second guess yourself when making changes.

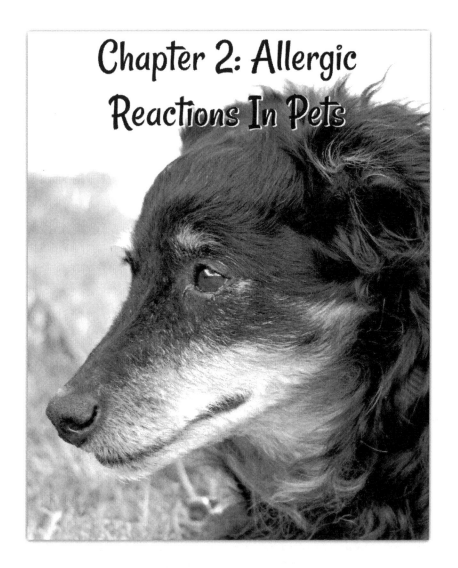

Chapter 2: Allergic Reactions In Pets

Chapter 2
Allergic Reactions in Pets

Normally allergies are caused from the overly processed same diet fed
for years. Diet is crucial as to what creates these allergies. Diet
change fixes allergy symptoms 80% of the time.

If you suspect or have had issues for awhile with your pets skin including hot spots, black gunk in the ears, yeasty ears and feet,

scratching, flaky skin, sneezing, coughing and/or watery eyes then read further on how to help your pet become allergy-free.

First off, eliminate all chemicals around the house. This includes laundry soaps, shampoos, lotions, medications, glass cleaners, air fresheners and anything you use that contains chemicals. Including burning candles. Get a diffuser instead (if you don't have cats). Learn about Essential oils before using. Use **chemical-free** fabric softener sheets (Meyer's) or better yet, purchase wool type dryer balls. Dryer sheets are hard on your dryer sensors anyway and may cause your dryer to fail. Use organic all-natural lawn fertilizers, no weed killers or bug sprays. There are many products available that do not contain chemicals and work just as well, if not better. Most all of your popular products contain a lot of chemicals. Think about your sheets, blankets, clothes, towels that are being washed in chemicals and you are lying on or wearing on your body. Your dog is right there with you. And your carpets, rugs and even your couch that may contain Scotchguard. Even in your vehicle.

Do not use ANY flea and tick medications you buy from your vet or from a pharmacy. Even the OTC (Over-The-Counter) junk you buy in stores is extremely toxic. I have seen/heard of many deaths from using these as well. Use all-natural treatments. Do **not** vaccinate your pets yearly. It is **not** needed. Rabies (by law) is to be given every 3 years. Make sure your vet is on the same page as this and offers the 3-year rabies vaccine and doesn't force pet parents to do the one-year vaccine. If he/she does, FIND A NEW VET. Ask for the Thimerosal-Free Rabies vaccine. I recommend titer testing for the other vaccines (Distemper etc). If your vet charges outrageous prices for titers, have him/her look into Vaccicheck. Check with Kansas State University and/or Dr. John Robb at ProtectThePets.com for titers on vaccines such as Rabies, Distemper and Parvo for $55. Or order other combo titers for Distemper, Parvo and Adenovirus titers through KSU. Do not let your vet take your dog to the back without you watching the vaccine being drawn up and injected if you decide on a vaccine. Some vets want to charge for both titers and vaccines. Don't get sucked into this. They should **not** ask you to pay for a vaccine if you paid for a titer.

For heartworm treatments or preventatives, use the all-natural solutions (see chapter on Heartworm Prevention and Treatment). Also add fragrant grasses in and around your yard that deter mosquitoes and insects. (Lavender, Lemongrass, Peppermint, Eucalyptus, etc.) For applications for your yard and to be added into foods, use Diatomaceous Earth (FOOD GRADE). Also D.E. kills and repels insects in your yard and home. It's a great dewormer as well. It does not kill tapeworms or heartworms. Pumpkin Seeds (can use raw powder as well) will kill tapeworms along with other parasites excluding heartworms. Give 1/4 teaspoon of pumpkin seed powder per 10 pounds of your dog's weight. It has also been said that Chamomile can work to prevent/expel both roundworms and whipworms.

If you would like to check for food allergies, you can do this through Dr. Jean Dodds. The test is around $300 at this time but it will hopefully give you answers. (Antigens/Foods being tested are beef, corn, duck, lentil, wheat, soy, cow's milk, lamb, venison, chicken, turkey, white fish, hen's egg, barley, millet, rice, oatmeal, salmon, rabbit, quinoa, potato, peanut, pork, and sweet potato). Not sure how accurate these are but it may help get you find a path.

Also make sure you have a thyroid check (T-4) as well. Stay completely away from grocery store or dept store pet treats and foods. These are made with lots of preservatives and chemicals. Learn to read ingredients when shopping. And when it comes to commercial pet foods, they are the number one problem in skin allergies and intolerances. These foods and treats contain so many chemicals, food dyes, preservatives, synthetic vitamins, and the 4Ds (Dead, Disabled, Dying, Diseased animals), all of which can make your pet sick. Maybe not for a while but eventually. Look into feeding a species-appropriate diet (raw). If you want results, you **must** make these changes.

Commercial pet foods are the lowest quality ingredients on our planet as you read in Chapter one. So your best bet is to steer completely away from pet foods. Feed a homemade diet with the much recommended supplements to help protect your dog's joints, organs and skin. If you want your pet to live a longer healthier life, this is the only way to go. Some commercial pet foods have also reported to even have killed pets or made then deathly sick and it took thousands of dollars to save that pet. It's like playing Russian Roulette with these commercial pet foods and treats.

There are many dogs that have had allergies to pet foods; let's say chicken, and the pet parent was unable to feed chicken flavored dog foods to their dog due to reactions. But many times when fed a raw diet, these allergies do not show up at all and therefore it means the dog is <u>not</u> and <u>never was</u> allergic to chicken. It was the commercial pet food; the way it is processed and the chemicals used on the ingredients that actually have caused the issues. In fact pet foods really do not contain much meat at all and what's in it is disgusting. Kibble is sprayed with rancid grease for taste as well. Who knows what's in that mix! If for some reason there is still a reaction to chicken in the raw diet, try organic. Regular chicken contains hormones, antibiotics and chemicals and that could be the problem. Yes it does; no matter what the package says. Organic chicken does not.

Giving dogs steroids constantly WILL shorten your dog's life. It is doing extensive damage to the organs every day they are used. DO NOT use these long term (over 2-3 weeks max) or regularly.

Steroids are a band-aid in a pill or injection form. They are not the solution! Neither is Apoquel. It's the new medication being handed out like candy by vets for allergies. This suppresses the immune system; not allowing it to do its job. You must remove the culprit that's causing the itching. This is not the solution, this is a big band-aid. Throw away the band-aid and allow the body to heal from within. Apoquel is killing dogs and making them very sick. It also causes cancer. Why put your dog through this when it isn't necessary? Yes you want to make your dog comfortable from all that scratching and sores, but you can do the same thing by changing the food you are feeding. Yes it takes some work, but isn't the end result worth it? Why allow both you and your dog to continue to be miserable!

Leaky Gut *(or Intestinal Permeability)*
Many times when there is so much havoc going on in the body, it can also be blamed on leaky gut. Leaky Gut Syndrome is the inability of the intestinal lining to prevent undigested food or potentially toxic

organisms from passing into the bloodstream. Leaky gut is caused by damage to the gut lining which allows abnormal absorption of bacteria, toxins and gut proteins, and leads to a large number of chronic conditions. Diseases that are said to be initiated or worsened by a leaky gut include environmental and food allergies, arthritis, inflammatory bowel disease (IBD), pancreatic disease and overgrowth of yeast.

It has been determined by holistic Drs that leaky gut is one of the causes of cancer. A connection has been found between the two. Leaky gut causes inflammation throughout the entire body wreaking havoc and causing different symptoms. This inflames all of the organs including weakening the immune system and allowing more disease and illness to attack.

Leaky gut starts out as allergy symptoms and progresses to malnutrition, and then it can create higher liver enzymes or other organ irregularities. Leaky gut should not be taken lightly and is one of the main causes in allergies. Chemicals and preservatives in foods can also contribute to leaky gut.
When leaky gut occurs, nutrients from foods do not get absorbed into the body. It leaks throughout holes in the digestive lining causing the body to react. Therefore you get your allergy symptoms.

Some of these symptoms include:

- Gas, Bloating, Diarrhea
- Vomiting
- Immune System Disorders
- Ear Infections
- Bad breath
- Gum disease
- Dry Eye
- Liver, Gallbladder and pancreatic disorders
- Joint pain
- Cancer
- Seizures
- Nutritional deficiencies

- Inflamed bladder
- Hyperactivity
- Skin rash, hot spots

NSAIDs and steroids are also known to cause Leaky Gut Syndrome as well as antibiotics. Remember, 70-80% of the immune system lives in the large intestine.

Once you make a diet change, you will need to help detox the body. You will need to use supplements to help it complete the detox process. Add in these recommended supplements:

- Probiotics
- Digestive Enzymes (higher doses)
- Fish oils (high quality sardine/anchovy, squid, or green lipped mussel)
- Vitamin E (non-soy) three times a week
- Organic Greens Powder or raw juiced/chopped green veggies
- Humic/Fulvic Acid
- Calcium (if not feeding raw bone daily)
- B-Complex
- Magnesium
- Quercetin (it acts like Benadryl-not to be given longer than 3 months)
- Milk Thistle
- Colostrum (organic or pasture-fed cows)
- Glutamine

If your dog has a sensitive stomach or intestinal tract issue, add Slippery Elm daily to help coat the lining of the tract. Slippery Elm along with Probiotics and Digestive Enzymes will help many allergies and tummy issues as well as leaky gut. Use Slippery Elm only for about 3 months at most. Then take it out of diet. If several months down the road you feel your dog needs it, it's ok to add it back in for a little while but do not give Slippery Elm daily long term.

To help remove heavy metals from the body that have been acquired through vaccines, unfiltered water, non-organic foods and other ways, you can use any of these:

- Activated Charcoal
- Chlorella
- Wheatgrass
- Moringa
- Dandelion Root
- Burdock Root
- Milk Thistle
- Diatomaceous Earth (Food Grade)

Leafy greens in general help remove these toxins.

Just add these in with wet foods. Activated Charcoal is well...black. So putting into food will turn it black and everything it touches. You may be able to have better luck using capsules. I use the powder in my doggie cookies I make.
Add coconut oil to the diet as well. You can also use it externally.

For immediate relief from itching and hot spots: Give a bath in Povidone Iodine and water. Dilute it to resemble a darker tea color. It's safe, non-toxic, antifungal, antibacterial, and anti-yeast. Soak for 2-5 minutes. Do not rinse off. Do this daily until itching stops or sores have subsided. Great for washing irritants off gathered from the lawn or other public places on those paws. You can find Povidone Iodine at any Pharmacy.

Until you make these changes, your dog will only become worse. It is inevitable that when all of these toxins enter the body that it eventually will no longer be able to fight off all the chemicals. So start immediately and make these changes not only for your dog but for your health as well. And also if you smoke, do NOT smoke anywhere around your pets at all. Take it outside and away from your pets. They cannot tell you that so I will.

Raw goat's milk is good for allergies. Pasteurized dairy of any kind is not. In fact pasteurization contributes to leaky gut as well. Fermented dairy is acceptable and tolerated.

Colloidal Silver
For ear infections, place 3 to 5 drops of Colloidal Silver into the ear canal 2 to 3 times a day. Gently rub/massage the ear in a circular motion till ear is saturated. Do not use any of this treatment if your dog's ear drums are perforated/punctured.
Apply to hot spots or insect bites 3 times daily with cotton ball or purchase the Colloidal Silver spray.

The best way to detox your dog is feed a homemade diet using as much organic foods as possible, filtering the water including the removal of fluoride and chlorine and a HEPA air filtration system in the home. You can get several air purifiers to put in your home especially at night where everyone sleeps. Diffusing essential oils will help as well.

Once you have changed the diet and added in probiotics and digestive enzymes, fish oils, vitamin E, filtered water, and cleared the house and yard of chemicals, you can then begin another form of detox. That's when you add in your greens, milk thistle and other items listed. Do all of this slowly. Add in one or two into the diet, then after 7 days; if there is no reaction; add in one or two more. Also start with lower dose and work up. Do not add everything in all at once or you may create a huge mess with the entire immune system. Your dog may get cannon butt and become one big ball of ITCH. It takes awhile to detox the body and you cannot hurry this. You must take it slow.

Signs of detox include:

- Mucous in poop
- Loose stools
- More scratching
- More hot spots
- Sneezing/watery eyes

You actually may experience numerous symptoms related to what you have already experienced with allergies and they may become more intense before it gets better. This is why we must detox the body slowly. So again, change the food, filter the water, remove chemicals inside and outside the house, remove toxins like flea and tick medications. Anything medication related for preventing heartworm, flea and tick and so on. All of these are chemicals in which can create reactions in the body.

Once you have done all of this and you are not having any intense reactions, this is when to add in your added supplements to finish cleansing the immune system. For severe conditions, I would detox for 6 months then off for 6 months then back on for 30 days. Do this every 6 months. Don't give up on getting through the detox part. It will be difficult especially the first time but if you take it slow, the symptoms will not be so severe. And next time it will be much easier and milder.

Pure Mangosteen Rind Juice
Mangosteen Juice has shown great promise in treating allergies in humans, it can also work equally well in treating animal diseases and symptoms of dogs allergies. The best way to help your dog with allergies is adding in Mangosteen Juice to your dog's diet.

Approximate Dosage:
Small dogs: 1 tsp
Medium dogs: 1 1/2 tsp
Large dogs: 2 tsp

Tip: Calendula oil is used for ear infections and infected anal glands. Dilute 10 drops into one cup of water for cuts and broken skin. Apply topically.

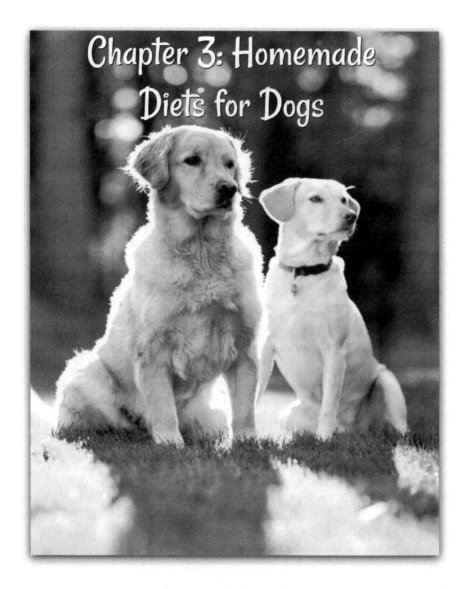

Chapter 3: Homemade Diets for Dogs

Chapter 3
Homemade Diets for Dogs

Starting a new diet change for your dog is exciting and nerve-racking, not knowing if you are ready or have all the information you need. Let me reassure you, it isn't as difficult as it may seem, nor is it as expensive as you may think. If you do your homework, you can have a workable budget and a happy, healthy dog. This article will be about my experiences with feeding raw; the transition of detoxing, and all the research I have done along the way.

First off, sit down with a pen and paper and do the math. How much a month do you spend on dog food, vet bills, vaccines, medications and anything else that pertain to caring for your dog? That includes prescription meds, heartworm preventatives, flea and tick meds etc.

To start off, you need to make a decision; are you going to fast your dog for 24 hours then jump right into raw or are you going to slowly transition? I know you may hear it's best to do it one way or the other. Honestly, I think you need to do what works best for you and your dog. (Puppies shouldn't fast. Just feed raw next meal). Always remember, anytime there is a change in diet, there will be a change in poop. Poop plays a huge role here in knowing what's going on, so learn to read the poop.

- Large stinky poop - kibble fed dogs
- Loose poop - detoxing, too many quick changes in diet
- Diarrhea - overloaded by all the changes in diet and supplements, slow down
- White poop - too much bone or calcium
- Small firm poop (with less odor) - just right

Look for a small freezer (used or new) to store raw foods in especially if you have large or multiple dogs. You will need the space.

Once you have decided how and when you will start, be prepared. First you will need supplements. You may hear many raw feeders say that dogs do not need added supplements when feeding a raw diet. This would be further from the truth. In the wild, when a wolf is eating its prey, they are gathering the needed nutrients. A wild rabbit to a wolf will be fresh meat that hasn't been laced with antibiotics and toxins. A cow when raised for slaughter is raised in very inhumane conditions. Yes this is what we humans are eating. So buying food from the grocery store is NOT your best selection for clean meats. Only when you run out of food at home or can't get your hands on other better raw foods is grocery store food acceptable.

Another decision to make here is what sort of raw will you feed? Whole prey (whole carcass), pieces of raw (chunks of meat fit for your size of dog) or ground raw. This book isn't about feeding dehydrated or commercial raw pet foods you buy in pet stores. Nor is it for whole prey diets. This is about gathering ingredients for a home-prepared raw diet. You have raw, freeze-dried/dehydrated that you can purchase in bags or chubs from the stores. You add water or cut a slice to feed. Most of these come with some (synthetic) vitamins but I can tell you, you will STILL need to add supplements, so why not know exactly what you are putting into your dog's food and adding in whole food forms of nutrients? You will spend more up front for supplements to gather a stock of what is needed but you get to pick them. Also know that commercial foods are much more costly.

Before starting your transition, I recommend a probiotic and digestive enzyme combo at least 5-7 days before changing foods. The longer the better on starting probiotics and digestive enzymes before making the diet change to help with the transition. If you have a puppy or a dog with allergies, add Colostrum into the daily diet as well. Once you have started your probiotics and digestive enzymes, try to see if your dog likes coconut oil. Put some on a spoon or finger and see if she/ he will eat it. Some dogs love it, some don't. You can always mix some in with the food. Start with a very small amount and increase a little bit as you go. Buy coconut oil that is unrefined extra virgin cold-pressed and in a glass jar. Normal amounts are 1/2 teaspoon per 20 lbs. If your dog doesn't seem to like the coconut oil at all and absolutely refuses to eat the food with it in it, try the **refined** coconut oil. It doesn't have that smell or flavor like unrefined although unrefined is much better but getting it in your dog is better than none at all. Also there is an MCT oil available. No smell or taste.
Stay away from plastics and cans of all foods as much as possible. Look for glass! Start with a very small amount and work up or you may get some loose stools.

I find the most confused newbie's are the ones that don't have something to look at (like a menu) to go by. It seems to make more sense when it is written down on like a recipe you would use for baking or cooking. It's like, I have this in my frig, can I feed this to my dog? Great question, let's find out. Starting out it seems extremely scary and overwhelming but don't let it be. It's not as difficult or confusing as it sounds. Plus you will have this book to come back to.

*DO NOT continue a long-term diet of kibble and raw. It confuses the digestive system. *Do NOT feed kibble and raw together at the same meal although I am seeing holistic vets recommend this. Not sure why as they know how the two digest differently.

First time feeding:
Use only one protein, chicken is usually the preferred protein to start. Feed a bland diet of chicken breasts with bone or alike for a couple of weeks. These can be ground up. After a couple weeks, you can add in organ meats. **Bone will make the poop firm; the organ meat will soften it.**

If your dog is allergic to chicken or poultry, start with rabbit or goat. Stick to one protein source for as long as needed (usually a couple of weeks) and monitor poops. If the first meal the dog gets with raw is chicken for example, feed chicken until poops return to normal: small and firm.

Percentages to feed per meal:
10% Bone
10% Organ (Offal)
80% Meat
Liver-1 oz per 10 lbs at least once a week. (Part of organ diet)

*Meats are high in phosphorus, bones are high in calcium.
** (Organ meats: liver, kidney, spleen, brain, testicles, and pancreas)

Fruits/Veggies: 5%-8% can be added daily on average.

Feeding times:
For young adults (over 6 months old) and mature adults– 1-2 meals per day. If 2 meals, then split amount.
For 4-6 months old - split into 3 meals per day.
For less than 4 months old - split into 4 meals per day.

While 2 meals a day have been recommended for as long as I remember, now it is being said to feed one meal a day. I think you know your dog and what is possible and works for you. So it's your choice. My dogs would eat my arm off if I fed them only once a day. Other dogs could care less.

Here is the break down in the amounts of food (for ex: 2.0 % of body weight):

1.5% – Overweight
2.0% – Average Activity (little outdoor time/2 or fewer walks a day)
2.5% – Above Average Activity (a few hours of activity per day)
3.0% – Average Activity with Weight Gain Goals
3.5 % – High Activity or Weight Gain Goals (Working Dogs)
4%+ –Puppies and Nursing or Pregnant bitches

The amounts vary and can always be adjusted up or down. It will be up to you to watch his/her weight and adjust it as needed. Some dogs will act as though they are starving. Just up the meat content a little. You can also add in veggies cooked or raw (juiced, steamed, or finely chopped). Raw chunks of veggies don't digest so you will need to help the dog out by juicing or chopping down into small fine pieces. Dogs have shorter digestive systems than us humans. Raw is best because they get the most nutrients. Buy organic if you can possibly afford it. Veggies and fruits have a high amount of GMOs along with pesticides so it is best to buy organic or you may be dealing with some issues with chemical reactions and even cancer, so buy organic if possible. This applies to EVERYTHING including eggs and supplements. Always buy organic and/or pasture-fed if you can. I have found some good prices even with organic supplements, and when adding supplements into the diet; don't just throw in the whole list of supplements and not expect issues with the poop or tummy upsets. Take it slow. Add supplements in a little at a time.
A couple for one week and if all goes well, add in a couple more the next week or so. Do this until you get them all going in. And start with low amounts and work up to recommended amounts.

Safe Protein Sources for Dogs

Muscle Meat
Beef
Lamb
Pork (Never feed your dog **fresh** raw pork as doing so can cause trichinosis - a parasitic disease caused by eating raw or undercooked pork. Make sure you freeze it 3 weeks prior to serving it raw. This also applies to wild game you may have hunted/killed or received from a friend).
Rabbit
Goat
Chicken
Turkey
Bison
Ox
Llama
Kangaroo
Ostrich
Duck
Pheasant
Quail
Venison
Buffalo

Meats high in fat: Lamb, Pork and Duck. Beef varies.

Organ Meats
Organ meats such as spleen, brain, kidney, eyeballs, ovaries, testicles, liver (especially liver) or any other secreting organ should also be included. Organs such as heart, lungs or other **non-secreting** organs are recognized as muscle meat. Organ meats are low in fat.

Green tripe (NOT bleached tripe found in grocery stores) is a great addition. It can be used to add weight gain and for added probiotics as well. Warning: It stinks! Put a clothes pin on your nose and keep going. Your dogs will love you for it.

If for some reason you run out of organ meat, they make a grass-fed organ mix in a capsule. It's called Ancestral Beef Organs. Nice product. This comes in capsules but you can open and sprinkle into food. Label recommends 6 capsules for human. I can't say exactly where the right amount for a dog would be, but 3 capsules will probably work just fine depending on your dog's size. This contains bovine liver, heart, kidney, pancreas and spleen. (FYI-Heart is a muscle meat, not considered an organ meat). If your dog gets diarrhea after giving this, back off on the amount given.

I try to give you options. Everyone has different work schedules and life styles and sometimes in a pinch, you can't carry around all this food/ supplements and sometimes you may not feel like it. I hope most days you can have time though to prepare your dogs food as it is as important as it is for your children. But having something to fall back on or make life a little simpler on some days is what we need to be ready for. So this is why I mention these alternate products.

Calf Liver:
Giving your dog raw liver once a week will supply it with all the vitamin A that it needs. Calf liver is one of the safest ways to give your dog vitamins A and B especially B-12, iron, Trace elements such as copper, zinc and chromium and COQ10. One ounce per 10 lbs at least once a week.

Fish (cooked or canned in water) *Buy low sodium*:
Anchovies
Salmon-Wild Pacific
Sardines
Shad
Smelt
Mackerel
Herring
Krill
Squid
Green Lipped Mussel oil
I use Iceland Pure sardine/anchovy oil because at this time it's the

only one I trust. If you can afford it, you may try Calamari oil from Dr. Peter Dobias. Another trustworthy product. The rest I pretty much do not trust.

Raw Fish

To feed or not to feed? Your decision. If you feed raw fish make sure it is wild caught. Farmed fisheries are not safe as it may contain flukes - a parasite that infests the liver. If you feed raw fish, freeze it for at least 3 weeks prior to feeding. I like feeding sardines packed in water that contains a low amount of sodium. Sodium is important to search out when buying all store-bought meats. Keep amounts minimal. Read the package. Look for under 110 milligrams (mg) of sodium. Small fish are best. Larger fish contain more mercury.

You can add a pinch of Himalayan Pink Sea Salt to food a couple times a week for minerals.

Fish oil vs. Flaxseed Oil

Technically flaxseed oil has omega-3, however, it doesn't have the DHA and EPA which is sorely missing from most diets and is crucial for your dog's health. Plus, it can be difficult for your dog to convert the ALA into needed DHA and EPA. You can make it easier for your dog to get these necessary omega-3 fatty acids with high quality fish oil for dogs. Calamari and Green Lipped Mussel oils work as well.

Seeds (always buy organic with nuts and seeds)

Flax Seeds - while Flax seeds are fine to give, I do not recommend them for omega-3 purposes or daily use without also using fish oils. These do not replace your fish oils. Fish oil is always needed. Do not give any Macadamia nuts. These are toxic to your dog. You can find more on this further down as you read. Nuts and seeds contain molds and mycotoxins unless organic. Is it really worth all that trouble? Just use fish oils.

Chia Seeds (organic only)

Two tablespoons of Chia seeds provide a 3-to-1 ratio of Omega-3 to Omega-6. Chia is non-allergenic. Look for milled and organic Chia seeds if possible. Chia seeds contain10 grams of fiber per two table-spoons.

You can use these when baking treats. Remember, these seeds will soak up a lot of water and create a gelatin effect so soak before feeding or serve up a smaller amount in wet foods so there isn't any possible choking when the moisture is absorbed. They also will need to be converted from ALA to DHA and EPA. This again is why I am partial to fish oils **only**. While seeds are nutritious, I wouldn't use unless baked in a treat.

Amount to use: 1/4 teaspoon for every 10 pounds of your dog's body weight. High amounts of omega-6 can cause diseases like arthritis so keep these amounts low. Keep all nuts to a minimum. A couple of organic raw pecans are fine but don't give any more than that at a time. Nuts can cause intestinal upset. My dogs like a few pecans on occasion.

Dairy Products
Limit all dairy to no more than twice a week. Pasteurized milk is not good for your dog. Raw milk helps with weakened immune systems and Kefir is a good source of protein and also a source of acidophilus which helps to prevent the overgrowth of bad bacteria in the digestive tract. You can make your own at home using either coconut milk or water grains. Look for organic grains. Homemade has stronger properties for healing and a much higher amount of probiotics. Plain organic yogurt is fine but Kefir is better.

Kefir or yogurt sweetened with sugar is not ideal for your dog. Kefir or yogurt sweetened with artificial sweeteners should be avoided AT ALL COSTS! Xylitol is especially dangerous for dogs and can result in liver damage and death even in small amounts.

*(Dairy products do not **replace** your probiotic and digestive enzymes supplements).*

Digestive enzymes also do much more than aid in digestion. They purify and cleanse the blood and remove toxins, parasites and fungus. Digestive enzymes also help boost the immune system. Cooking also destroys digestive enzymes, so it is important that your dog gets extra digestive enzymes and probiotics to help aid digestion especially with sensitive tummies, leaky gut or allergy issues.

Acceptable Dairy (organic):
Plain Cottage Cheese
Plain Yogurt
Plain Kefir or homemade Kefir milk
Raw goats milk (pasture-fed)

(Yes it's ok to give them a bite of raw/organic cheese now and then-wink)
I do not recommend canned foods due to the BPA lining in the cans. Even if it says BPA Free, it will contain BPS. It is 10 times as toxic as BPA. There is no winning with the cans. So avoid if at all possible. Use frozen or fresh organic.

I recommend veggies (raw preferably-juiced/finely chopped) to gather as many nutrients as possible. A small amount can be added to each diet. If you don't want to spend much time in the kitchen preparing veggies, you can add in an organic greens powder. It is full of nutrients and it's easy to add into ground raw foods. It does have a strong flavor and smell so you may need to mask it using something your dog likes. Some dogs are not bothered by this powder and others are. Get to know your dog's new likes with this new diet. You can try organic Chlorella, Moringa or Kale powders instead. Also a good mineral supplement is Humic/Fulvic Acid. It's all-natural. Find what works for you and your schedule. Some people have plenty of time to prepare an entire meal, others work full-time and the last thing they want to do is be in the kitchen all night. So to make it simple, add the greens powder and supplements and that will help keep it balanced. Also try preparing meals that will last for a week so that on your busy days, you can just plop it on a plate and feed. I like to add in my powders and also throw in a tablespoon of raw organic chopped kale into the mix.

If you choose to cook the veggies, that's ok just make sure they get their supplements for the day. Cooked foods do not need to be juiced. You can also steam the veggies and more nutrients are retained.

Fruits (organic):
Apples
Apricots *(Apricot seeds are great to be used for a cancer treatment and preventative). (See Cancer Prevention/Treatment Chapter)*
Avocado is OK for dogs. *The pit and skin of the avocado is toxic and should never be consumed by dogs.*
Bananas
Blackberries
Blueberries *(antioxidant -great for cancer prevention and treatment, and an immune system builder)*
Cantaloupe
Cherries (remove the pit)
Cranberries
Coconut
Kiwi
Mango
Peaches (remove the pit)
Pears
Pineapple
Plums
Raspberries
Strawberries
Watermelon
Citrus (such as lemon, lime, oranges, grapefruit) in very small amounts.

When buying fruits, buy organic only and frozen is even better. I am hearing some brands of organic strawberries are not organic. Sometimes we just need to research this stuff. Try frozen organic if you like.
Some people may think that giving a dog fruit and/or vegetables will give the dog diarrhea. They actually provide high quality soluble fiber and help prevent diarrhea and constipation.

Soluble fibers attract water and form a gel, which slows down digestion thereby delaying the emptying of the stomach and makes a dog feel full, which helps to control a hungry pooch and keep the weight down. Slower stomach emptying can also have a beneficial effect on controlling blood sugar levels and insulin sensitivity, which helps control diabetes. Keep fruits to a minimum though.

I find blueberries or any of your berries to be some of the best fruits to add. They are loaded with antioxidants and are great immune boosters. In the summer make some frozen treats using berries. Yogurt and blueberry frozen in ice cube trays or alike. If your dog doesn't like cold treats, serve up some room temp berries mixed in cottage cheese, kefir or yogurt. You can even add into their foods.

Vegetables (organic-raw chopped, cooked or raw pureed):
Alfalfa Sprouts
Asparagus
Broccoli
Kale
Spinach (limit or avoid in dogs prone to kidney/bladder stones)
Brussels Sprouts
Cauliflower
Celery
Cucumber
Green Beans (Limit amount. Can cause stones in higher amounts for dogs prone to stone formation)
Squash
Sugar Snap Peas (in the pod or out)
Green Peas
Zucchini
Sweet Potatoes (high in carbs - limit amounts)
Yams (high in carbs - limit amounts)
Carrots (raw carrot juice has been used in cancer patients as well)
Spinach (while spinach is safe to feed, too much spinach can cause kidney/bladder stones)

Spinach is included in the Starwest Botanicals Greens Power that I recommend so if your dog has a history of kidney or bladder stones, try using Organic Kale, Organic Chlorella or Organic Moringa.

- Finely chop fruits/vegetables - either by hand or with a food processor/blender/juicer
- Lightly steam vegetables

Grains:

Grains are not part of a dog's natural diet; here are some important points to note. I recommend removing all grains from your dog's diet.

If you must keep grain in your dog's diet:
Make sure that you only provide your dog with human quality grains and ONLY organic in small amounts! Otherwise grains contain aflatoxins and can cause liver cancer. Grains absorb liquid, so ingesting uncooked grains that have not been pre-soaked can lead to swelling and bursting of the stomach; dangerous at the least, lethal at worst.
I do not recommend grains in diets at all. They cause too many serious problems especially in larger dogs. So do not feed grains or high carbs like white potatoes or rice.

Grains can be completely replaced by substituting a combination of sweet potato, chickpeas and lentils.

Calcium (Important)

One of the most common mistakes that people make when feeding a home-cooked diet is not adding in calcium. You must add calcium when you feed a diet that does not include bones. Adult dogs need around 800 to 1,000 mg of calcium per pound of food fed.

The ideal Calcium: Phosphorus ratio in the canine diet is between 1:1 and 2:1. Meat contains a lot of phosphorus, so the more meat a diet contains, the more calcium will be required to reach the correct calcium: phosphorus ratio. Adding 800 to 1,000 mg of calcium will provide the correct calcium: phosphorus ratio even for a high-meat diet, unless you use a calcium supplement that also contains phosphorus. In that case, moderately higher amounts of calcium may be needed to balance out the additional phosphorus contained in the supplement.

Ground eggshell can be used as a calcium supplement. Rinse eggshells and dry them on a counter overnight, or in the oven, then grind them in a clean coffee grinder. One large eggshell provides one teaspoon of ground eggshell, which contains 2,000 mg of calcium. Don't use eggshells that haven't been ground to powder, as they may not be absorbed as well.

I recommend powdered calcium you can use in place of above - powdered seaweed calcium or powdered eggshell calcium although I prefer the eggshell most.

Calcium and phosphorus must be in balance. Calcium deficiencies sometimes brought on by high meat diets and no bone, as meat contains phosphorus can result in nervousness, lameness, muscle spasms, heart palpitations, eczema, decrease in bone density, osteoporosis, gum erosion, increased cholesterol levels, seizures, hemorrhages, arthritis, and bone fractures. For dogs, supplement high amounts of calcium only in the first year of life, or during pregnancy and nursing, as too much can cause kidney stones (use vitamin C along with calcium to prevent this). Also add in Magnesium Citrate to avoid all types of stones and to treat oxalate stones. Dogs deficient in magnesium has been known to cause stone formation.

Calcium-eggshell or seaweed
Approximate dosage or follow label and/or see above under calcium:
0-25 lbs: 1/4-1/2 teaspoon
25-50 lbs: 1/2-1 teaspoon
50-75 lbs: 1-1 1/2 teaspoon
75+ lbs: 1 1/2-2 teaspoon

Raw Eggs
Make sure you wash the eggshell before cracking open if fresh off the farm. Some people advise that dogs should not be given raw eggs due to the chance of salmonella poisoning. It is also true that a dog's stomach acids are stronger than a human's and a dog produces more bile than a human does. While dogs are better at fighting salmonella than humans, dogs still can get salmonella poisoning, but they can tolerate higher levels of salmonella than we can. If you want to be on the safe side you can cook your dog's egg (poached, scrambled, boiled). Feed the whole egg. Feeding the white of the egg only can cause a vitamin deficiency.

Organic and/or pasture-fed; no more than twice a week if you choose to feed these. Once a week is preferred especially if raw. If you have access to farmed eggs, make sure the chickens are pasture-fed only and not fed grains such as GMO corn.

NOTE: Garlic is safe in smaller amounts and not to be given daily. In large doses, Garlic (like onions) can cause oxidative damage to red blood cells, creating Heinz bodies and making the body reject these cells from the bloodstream. If large doses are ingested on a regular basis, the process can lead to Heinz-body anemia and even death.

Most dogs adjust to a quick transition, one night its kibble for dinner, the next day they have a raw breakfast. Others need a fasting period of 24 hours and never do this longer than one meal with puppies. Do not mix kibble and raw, as the time it takes to digest kibble is far longer than it takes to digest raw sometimes resulting in a stomach upset. Canned organic 100% pumpkin is great to have on hand to help any upset tummies and great for constipation and diarrhea.

Has your dog has been eating kibble all of its life? Kibble is full of a lot of unnatural ingredients like preservatives, artificial flavors, food colorings, chemical toxins, synthetic vitamins and minerals. When switching to a healthy diet, the body may begin to detox causing allergic symptoms. Don't panic, it's all part of nature. The body is cleansing itself. Give it a couple of weeks to adjust and cleanse. Once you have gotten through this process, add in organic Milk Thistle powder to this (5 days on, 2 days off weekly for 1-3 months.). This will help cleanse the liver (See Chapter 2-Allergic Reactions In Pets). Give this for several months until you have completely transitioned your dog using at least 4 different proteins.

Detox every 6 months for 2 - 4 weeks to rid the toxins your dog is still getting. Toxins come from breathing in air, drinking water if not filtered, medications, vaccines, chemicals in yard(s) and house. (Wash off feet after walking on neighbors grass or other public areas. Use apple cider vinegar and water.) You can't avoid everything but also start looking into making changes in these areas as well for the future to reduce the amount of exposure.

While your dog is transitioning, you may see excess shedding, dry skin, runny eyes, and mucus in the poop, or perhaps dried up white poop a day or so later. The white is the bone content in the diet. You can reduce calcium if you are giving it. Keep bones at the recommended dosage. White poop is a sign your dog is getting enough calcium and you can reduce the intake of calcium. You may see the poop becoming smaller in size and less of it. The smell will be less. Your dog may not drink as much water as normal. Raw diets are full of water content so your dog won't require as much water as the dehydrating cardboard kibble. Also during the transition, you may see your dog showing some skin conditions. If it is mild, apply coconut oil onto the dog's skin and/or half (water) and half Apple Cider Vinegar. You will want to use raw unfiltered "mother" ACV. If there is itching involved, bathe your dog in Povidone Iodine and water (dark tea color). Do not rinse off, pat dry. Colloidal Silver works as well for a topical for skin lesions.

 Unrefined virgin organic coconut oil is a wonderful addition to any diet. You can use internally and externally. Internally don't go overboard; start off with a smaller amount, 1/4-1/2 teaspoon and work your way up depending on your dog's size. Less for tiny/small dogs. The situation will resolve itself with time, (generally a week or two, but up to a couple months in some cases) as new cells must replace older ones in order for the detox process to be completed. If your dog can't stand the taste, try using the "refined" organic coconut oil. If all is going well after a couple of weeks, try a new protein like goat, venison, beef or rabbit. You can feed chicken necks once a week. Also skinless/boneless low sodium sardines in water, low sodium salmon (Trader Joe's has a very low sodium pink salmon and they also have some low sodium sardines although I found some lower made by Season Brand and Wild Planet. Wal-Mart and Costco's carry the Season Brand in some of their stores.) You can feed organic cottage cheese once a week or add a little bit of organic plain kefir to the food or serve alone for an additive. Cottage cheese is like a dessert for my dogs. It's not a necessity. It's more for adding in something different and tasty. You can do so many things. Keep it interesting for your dog. Change up the meals. Do NOT feed the same protein day in and day out once you establish the transition, which may take a couple of months. Your dog WILL get sick. This is unhealthy. Feeding the same type of food every day will make your dog unhealthy. We need to balance the diet so rotate at least 4 proteins. Your dog will probably stop drinking as much water as raw meats contain a lot of moisture. This doesn't apply to a cooked diet so much.

Do not feed pits of fruits and no grapes (grape seeds are safe), raisins, onions, or chocolate.(Carob in place of chocolate is safe and acceptable). Learn what is safe to feed and what isn't. Watch out for Xylitol in peanut butters and other human foods. It's in toothpastes as well so do not use human toothpastes on your dog. Xylitol is very toxic even in small amounts. I have created a wonderful toothpaste and rinse to help fight gum disease and bacteria in the mouth.

For fighting gum disease, I have created a special recipe for brushing your dog's teeth and providing an oral rinse to fight bacteria.

- 1 teaspoon of Coconut oil
- 1 teaspoon of Baking soda (can substitute with Diatomaceous Earth-Food Grade)
- 1/2 teaspoon of filtered Chlorine and Fluoride-free water to help form a paste (if needed)

Brush using your dog's own tooth brush. Soft bristled. Or use a finger brush. You can also use an electric tooth brush with your dog's own brush, whatever your preference.

After brushing
Mix one capsule (or 1/2 teaspoon of powder) of probiotics with filtered Chlorine and Fluoride-free water. Pour into a syringe for oral administration. Squirt this liquid around your pet's teeth and gums. This will also help fight bacteria and any yeasty problems in the mouth. Do this with each brushing. Following these steps will reduce your build up of tartar and bacteria.
Colloidal Silver also works as well. You can brush the teeth using Colloidal Silver. Helps prevent tarter build up. No need to dilute when brushing. Get yearly teeth cleanings as well if needed (or feed meaty bones 3 times a week like a rib bone). Keep the teeth clean and free from tarter build up and bacteria. Give probiotics to your dogs (add into food) weeks before, during and after a teeth cleaning to help reduce bacteria from spreading.
As for raw bones, they are wonderful for cleaning teeth. A raw rib bone 2-3 times a week will keep the teeth fairly clean. Although you

may need a teeth cleaning eventually depending on your dog. Just keep an eye on the teeth and brush as often as possible. Daily is recommended. Some dogs have more teeth issues than others, certain breeds like Chihuahuas, Dachshunds etc. Clean teeth are important to your dog's health. If you have rotten, loose, tarter buildup or failing teeth, these can cause more bacteria in which can spread throughout the body causing organ failure so a clean mouth is very important to your dog's health. Just ask your vet to skip the fluoride with the cleaning. Yep vets use this on our pets too.

Do not feed cooked bones at all. Cooked bones are dangerous. Also stay away from the weight-bearing bones. They can break teeth. Marrow bones can also be dangerous like getting stuck on the snout or bottom jaw. Always supervise your dog when they have bones. Chicken necks are soft and easily to chew and digest. Only feed once or twice a week at most on the necks. They are soft so they don't clean the teeth as well since the bones are smaller. Chicken feet are good as well and loaded with glucosamine. Turkey necks are larger and may cause an issue with smaller dogs or fast-eating dogs when swallowing. (Feed with caution until you get to know your dog). I recommend chicken necks until you get better acquainted with feeding raw bones. I do not recommend pork bones of any kind. Only finely ground in raw foods.

As for feeding pork, there is a lot of debate on whether to feed pork or not. Pork is fine to feed but make sure it has been frozen for 3 weeks prior to feeding it to your dog. Same goes for wild game that you may have killed in the wild. That also includes raw fish. I myself don't recommend feeding raw fish but if you do, freeze it for 3 weeks prior to feeding. Pork is higher in fat so if your dog has a history of pancreatic inflammation, don't feed pork, lamb or duck and limit your beef. Clean up is easy. Clean as you would after you prepare to cook your meats for yourself. You handle raw chicken, hamburger, steak, pork, prime rib etc. You clean up after your family. Same applies to raw dog food diets.

Make sure you use digestive enzymes and probiotics if your dog has pancreatic inflammation. (Give anti-inflammatory herbs as well for the inflammation.) You may need to triple the amount of probiotics and digestive enzymes if a normal dose isn't working. Make sure you feed small meals and limit treats etc.

While you are transitioning, don't lose hope if your dog isn't taking to it as well as you think she/he should. Sometimes it can take a couple months to get your dog accustomed to eating a different diet but eventually they will get the hang of it. It is always the pet parent that gives up before they should. Give it time. If something isn't working, try something different. Add a little cooked chicken or chicken broth or bone broth on top of the raw food. For newly fed raw diets, you can try searing small bite size pieces of meat before feeding. This may also help your dog transition. Add some sardines in the mix.

The thing for you to do is to look for a nearby co-op or buy from a source online or local. Go to the Farmers Market for great deals. I myself buy from a supplier and the shipping is low considering it is being shipped with ice and it is delivered right to my doorstep so no heavy loading and unloading my vehicle of meats. And they tell the meat/bone/organ ratio so it makes it much simpler for me.

 According to the size of your dog or how many mouths you have to feed as to what it will cost you per month. It costs me almost double the amount to feed a premium canned food than what I pay for raw. Canned still is over-processed, contains those unknown ingredients (listed in Chapter 1) and contains synthetic vitamins.

You are probably wondering why I like to add veggies when you may have heard raw diets do not need them. I do consider dogs carnivores, but if you can add a few raw veggies to add whole food nutrients, then that's why I recommend them. But some pet parents don't want to puree or chop up raw veggies so I recommend the greens powders. You can buy pre-chopped frozen veggies in stores if you look. I even add a little organic carrot juice at times and Fulvic/Humic acid. You can always take an afternoon one day and make all the veggie servings needed for the week and freeze/store them until time to feed. And to back up my recommendations, these comments come from some of the best holistic vets out there.

"It is no longer a question if a diet without supplements is complete. The question is what is missing. No matter what diet you feed, it is likely to be depleted of some nutrients because of worldwide mineral and nutrient soil depletion. ~ Dr. Dobias"

"The best of diets – even a raw, species-specific diet – can come from soils that are depleted or from lower quality food sources. Sometimes the food simply loses many of its nutrients through processing and storage. And most commercially available pet foods, even if they're "fortified" to meet AAFCO standards, contain synthetic, lab-concocted vitamins and minerals which don't provide optimum nutrition."~ Dr. Karen Becker

And when it comes to fur and feathers, here is what Dr. Becker has to say:
"Protein quality is extremely variable. There are highly assimilable and digestible proteins (proteins your pet's body can easily absorb and make use of), and there are proteins that are wholly indigestible. For example beaks, feet, hides, tails and snouts are 100 percent protein, but all 100 percent is indigestible.
All protein has a biologic value, which is its usable amino acid content. Eggs have the highest biologic value at 100 percent. Fish is a close second at 92 percent. Feathers, as you might guess, have zero biologic value. They are all protein, but they are neither digestible nor assimilable." ~ Dr. K. Becker

Let's Get Started
Day One Feeding Raw:

Day 1 of starting (after you have already started probiotics and digestive enzymes preferably at least a week before):

(If allergic to poultry; try rabbit or goat. If your dog has allergies to chicken, it may be best to avoid all poultry for several months)

- Chicken with bone (ground or small bites-no skin)
- Pureed or finely chopped raw veggies with some fruits (fruits are optional)

- Apple Cider Vinegar (1 teaspoon-1 TBSP depending on size of dog)
- Fish oil/Krill oil/Calamari oil and/or low-sodium sardines in water (Wild Planet and Season Brand has the lowest sodium content. Trader Joe's also has a low sodium one).
- Probiotics/Digestive Enzymes
- Add Calcium (if not 10% bone in diet)

Day 2:
- Chicken with bone (ground or small bites-no skin)
- Pureed or finely chopped raw veggies
- Apple Cider Vinegar (1 teaspoon-1 TBSP depending on size of dog)
- Fish oil/Krill oil/ Calamari oil and/or low-sodium sardines in water
- Coconut oil (1/4-1/2 teaspoon per 20 lbs)
- Probiotics/Digestive Enzymes
- Add Calcium (if not 10% bone in diet)

You will need to add in Vitamin E (non-soy) three times a week along with fish oils. This is important. Dry E Succinate is best. Soy can be hidden in labels (mixed tocopherols).

Alternate these days for 14 days. If all is going well the first week still using same protein, add in organ meats for another 7 days. This may cause some loose stools. Keep an eye on the poop. Loose stools or even mucus in stools is not a bad thing; it's adjusting and releasing toxins. But if you ever have runny diarrhea, stop organs immediately. This isn't normal for diarrhea but loose stools are. Add in some 100% organic pumpkin to the diet or you may have to fast your dog for a day to resume back to feeding meat and bone only if diarrhea occurs. If it does, wait till poop returns to normal then add in tiny bits of organ meat and gradually work up over a 7 day period. Some systems are more delicate than others so you have to go much slower than normal. You will get there, just be patient. You can also double the amount of digestive enzymes and probiotics for awhile until the system adjusts and calms down and is doing beautifully.

If your dog is doing wonderful and not having any issues at all, try a new protein for example like beef or rabbit.

Feed:
Beef (80%)/organs (10%)/bones (10%) for 7 days along with the recommended supplements you have been using from day one.
If everything is going well (nice firm poop), after 7 days switch to Turkey (80%)/organs (10%)/bones (10%).

After 7 days of doing well, you can try a new protein. If all 4 have worked well with only minor bumps in the road, time to start adding in some things.

If loose stools, cut out organ meat until poop is firm again, then slowly add organs back in.

Permanent Menu/Recipe:
Your protein choice with bone and organ meats (see feeding schedule - once or twice a day for adult dogs) Alternate 4 proteins.
Pureed or finely chopped raw veggies with some fruits (or greens powder) daily or every other day. *(See Chapter on Supplements and dosing if not listed below)*

Add in or continue with these added nutrients:

- Humic/Fulvic Acid (daily or every other day)
- Probiotics/Digestive enzymes daily
- Fish oil/Krill oil/ Calamari oil and/or low sodium sardines in water daily
- Calf Liver (1 oz per 10 lbs) once a week
- Add Calcium (Daily if you don't have 10% bone)
- Vitamin E (non-soy) three times a week

Optional or can be given once or twice a week or alternated. These are just extras for variety.
- Plain Kefir (1 teaspoon-1 TBSP depending on size of dog) couple times a week
- Plain Cottage Cheese once a week (for added flavor to a meal)

- Raw or cooked egg 1-2 times a week
- Chicken feet (full of glucosamine) once a week
- Chicken necks once a week
- Low sodium sardines in water-twice a week
- Canned low sodium pink salmon (Check Trader Joe's for best) once a week or less. Most are high in sodium so use sparingly. Avoid if your dog has heart disease.

Foods dogs cannot/should not have or are toxic:
- Chocolate
- Green Tomatoes
- Grapes (skins and meat) (seeds are fine)
- Raisins
- Xylitol (found also in some peanut butters and other foods)
- Rhubarb
- Onions/onion powder
- Yeast dough
- Sugar
- Salt (Himalayan pink sea salt is acceptable-a pinch) NO table salt!
- Cinnamon-Cassia (Acceptable is Ceylon Cinnamon)
- Macadamia nuts - can cause bladder stones if you give to your dog regularly. They also can affect the muscular and skeletal systems and cause hindquarter paralysis in some dogs if fed long-term. All nuts that are given to dogs should be ORGANIC ONLY due to mycotoxins.

For Treats: You can make your own dehydrated chicken or beef (any type of meats you would normally feed) jerky strips or bake some gluten free cookies for your dog. I make my own treats and use organic buckwheat (fruit) flour and add in some carob, greens powder, herbs, activated charcoal, and ginger. Also some organic coconut flakes. I throw in different flavored things to keep it interesting for my dogs. You can also buy some that are grain-free and organic from small mom and pop shops. Also see a good list on my website of the Top Best Dog Treats for ordering.

Here is a quick reference chart

Week One	Week Two	Week Three +
Chicken with bone/no skin/ground or small bites. Add Calcium (if not 10% bone in diet)	Chicken with bone/no skin/ground or small bites. Add Calcium (if not 10% bone in diet)	Goat with bone - ground or small bites. Add Calcium (if not 10% bone in diet) Alternate protein every week.
Finely chopped raw veggies (pick 1-2 at a time)	Finely chopped raw veggies (pick 1-2 different ones at a time)	Finely chopped raw veggies (your preference) 5-8% veggies
Apple Cider Vinegar (1 teaspoon-1 TBSP depending on size of dog)	Apple Cider Vinegar (1 teaspoon-1 TBSP depending on size of dog)	Apple Cider Vinegar (1 teaspoon-1 TBSP depending on size of dog)
Fish oil/Krill oil/Calamari oil and/or low-sodium sardines in water	Fish oil/Krill oil/Calamari oil and/or low-sodium sardines in water.	Fish oil/Krill oil/Calamari oil and/or low-sodium sardines in water .
Probiotics/Digestive Enzymes (Double dose for 30 days)	Probiotics/Digestive Enzymes (Double dose for 30 days)	Probiotics/Digestive Enzymes (Double dose for 30 days)
Coconut oil (1/4 teaspoon per 20 lbs) Alternate every other day	Coconut oil (1/4-1/2 teaspoon per 20 lbs) Alternate every other day	Coconut oil (1/4-1/2 teaspoon per 20 lbs) Can alternate every other day or daily
Do not feed cooked bones	Add Vitamin E - 3 times a week	Add Vitamin E - 3 times a week
Cooked egg 1-2 times a week (boiled, poached, or scrambled)	Cooked egg 1-2 times a week (boiled, poached, or scrambled)	Cooked egg 1-2 times a week (boiled, poached, or scrambled)
No organ meat at this time	No organ meat at this time	Add organ meats if poop is normal. (Spleen, brain, kidney, eyeballs, ovaries, testicles, calf liver (1 oz per 10 lbs) once a week) 10% total

Chicken necks and chicken feet 1-2 times a week. Chicken hearts for added Taurine.	Chicken necks and chicken feet 1-2 times a week. Chicken hearts for added Taurine.	Chicken necks and chicken feet 1-2 times a week. Chicken hearts for added Taurine.
If allergic to chicken, start with goat or rabbit (meat and bone only)	Himalayan Pink Sea Salt couple times a week for minerals (a dash)	Himalayan Pink Sea Salt couple times a week for minerals (a dash)
No added supplements at this time	Add in Fulvic/Humic Acid	Add in supplements (2 at a time for 3 days at least) Then two more and so on.
Feed raw bones such as rib bones for chewing 2-3 times a week		Can add an organic dairy listed from book at this time once a week.

For problems in transitioning:
While this is extremely rare, if your dog's body goes into complete chaos, then stop the diet, fast the dog for 24 hours, then start again by cooking the food first. (Actually you may want to start with bone broth for a day to ease back into the diet.) Cook the food for a couple of weeks, then as your dog gets use to cooked foods, start slowly backing away from it being completely cooked. Cook it half way. Cut into small pieces if needed. Feed for a couple weeks like that. Then try cooking it less each time till you are able to get to raw only. Some dogs may transition this way much easier as well. Sometimes you have to trick the dog because they are smart little critters. Most all dogs love cooked foods but they will obtain more nutrients from raw so try to get to that point if possible. Even if you sear them from now on, at least they are getting some form of raw.
If any loose stools, diarrhea or constipation, add some canned 100% pumpkin to the diet (1/2 teaspoon per 10 lbs). If any occasional vomiting (no more than 2-3 times overall), you can add in Slippery Elm daily for a month or so for sensitive tummies.

Bully Sticks
Some say these are bad and some say good. Let me explain this. I recently read where a well known holistic vet mentioned to their

followers not to feed bully sticks due to the bacteria. My mouth dropped and I had to laugh. Really? Ok, you have bacteria in raw meats; you have bacteria in kibble foods and canned foods. In fact most contaminated food is commercial pet foods. Just always remember, anytime you handle any type of foods, human foods, pet foods, raw foods, bully sticks, treats and alike, always wash your hands with soap and water after handling. That's it. It's that simple. *Some bully sticks are hard and may break or chip teeth. Use with caution.*

Do not give store bought rawhide bones or alike. These are dangerous and there are many horrible gut wrenching reports of deaths from these.

Now for supplements, I have created a list of what you will need. See next chapter on supplements and dosage amounts as well. These supplements can be tweaked along the way. But for now, it's a great list to start with and provide with daily meals.

Calcium-eggshell or seaweed (if not feeding 10% bone)
Approximate dosage or follow label:
0-25 lbs: 1/4 - 1/2 teaspoon
25-50 lbs: 1/2 - 1 teaspoon
50-75 lbs: 1 - 1 1/2 teaspoon
75+ lbs: 1 1/2 - 2 teaspoon

Fish oils (needed): (Krill, Squid or Anchovy and Sardine)
Always buy high quality fish oils. You will find many oils out there but not of good quality and therefore are rancid or loaded with mercury. Follow dosing on bottle. Buy in glass or metal containers. NO plastic due to BPA/BPS. Calamari (squid) oil is a great oil as well. *Stop fish oil and Vitamin E approximately seven days before surgery.*

The areas with the highest contamination levels include most of the Atlantic Ocean, the Gulf of Mexico, the Chesapeake Bay, the waters around Northern Europe and China. These are areas that have been industrialized for many years. The waters surrounding New Zealand are some of the cleanest on the planet. Industrialization is mostly limited to the North Island. The waters are far away from major shipping lanes. The government has many regulations in place that help to protect the environment, prevent pollution and ensure that the fish populations are sustainable. Krill and Wild Salmon oil contains some form of Astaxanthin. Astaxanthin is a powerful antioxidant. Antioxidants help protect your pet's cells from free radical damage. Needed especially in older dogs.

Follow label or:
Daily Dose:
Small dogs (up to 30 lbs): 250 - 500mg
Medium dogs (31-50 lbs): 750 - 1000mg
Large dogs (51-80 lbs): 125 - 1500mg
Giant dogs (81+ lbs): 1700 - 2000mg

Greens Powder (if not adding in veggies)
Ingredients in Starwest Botanicals Greens Powder:
Organic barley grass, organic wheat grass, organic spirulina, organic spinach, organic alfalfa leaf, organic kelp, organic dulse leaf, organic barley grass juice, organic orange peel, organic beet root, organic dandelion leaf, organic lemon peel, organic ginkgo leaf, and organic wheat grass juice.

Dosage:
Small dogs: 1/4-1/2 teaspoon
Medium/Large dogs: 1/2-1 teaspoon
Giant dogs: 1-1 1/2 teaspoons

Greens contain some of your highest amount of vitamins. In today's world even the best grown organic veggies and fruits are lacking in higher content of vitamins and minerals due to our depleted soils. Same for our meats. In a perfect world we wouldn't need extra supplementation but because of our meats lacking due to over-use of antibiotics and medications and poor diets fed to the cows and chickens and other animals we consume, we must add extra food sources. Although dogs are carnivores, giving a small amount of veggies or greens powder can have huge benefits for your dog due to what is lacking in our foods and especially our meats. Greens (leafy) have your best sources for vitamins. If your dog doesn't want to eat the organic mixed greens blend, I recommend trying organic Kale,

Moringa, or Chlorella powders. "Amazing Grass - The Original" is a good brand and doesn't has as strong of a smell.

Note: Dogs low in iodine can have signs of aggression, fear of noises and weight gain. Kelp has a high amount of iodine so be very careful with it. Dulse is a much lower content of iodine and is much safer to use even in higher amounts. Dulse also contains manganese.

Raw Unfiltered Apple Cider Vinegar with "Mother"
Dosage:
0-25 lbs: 1 teaspoon
25-50 lbs: 2 teaspoon
50-75 lbs: 1 TBSP
75+ lbs: 1 1/2-2 TBSP

ACV is known for maintaining the acid/alkaline balance of the digestive tract. If you have a dog that has clear, watery discharge from the eyes, runny noses, or coughs with a liquid sound, use ACV in his or her food. ACV works well against yeast. If your dog has the itchies, add into food. You can use a few drops in his or her ears after cleaning them to avoid ear infections. Apple cider vinegar is also known for its antibacterial and anti-fungal properties. Works well for yeast in the body and adjusting the PH levels as well. Add to diet for cancer patients.

Vitamin E (needed 3 times a week): Vitamin E (Dry E Succinate-soy free) is a powerful antioxidant that plays a crucial role in support-ing pet health. Pet food alone does not contain enough vitamin E to meet your dog's needs. Supplementing your dog's diet with natural vitamin E can help prevent serious health problems created by vita-min E deficiency. It is a must especially when giving fish oils. Most of your vitamin E supplements contain soy. Avoid soy in all products. I found Dry E Succinate doesn't contain it in most incidences and comes recommended by holistic Drs. Do not give softgels to dogs. They go in one end and out the other without dissolving.

Dosage:
Vitamin E amounts:
Small dogs: 200IU

Med/Large dogs: 300-400IU
Giant dogs: 600IU
(Do not go over this dosage)

Coconut oil (recommended): Coconut oil (organic unrefined virgin) aids allergies, skin issues such as dry skin and hair, ear infections, yeast build up, healing wounds or sores. (Trader Joe's carries a good one in a glass jar as well as Kroger's brand (Simple Truth-Organic) Look for glass jars. Remember, plastic contains BPA like cans. Coconut oil is considered an antibacterial, antiviral and anti-fungal agent. This is considered a healthy fat.

Dose: 1/4-1/2 teaspoon per 10 lbs.
Start with smaller amounts and work up to recommended dosage. Coconut oil aids allergies, skin issues such as dry skin and hair, ear infections, yeast build up, and healing of wounds and sores. You can use internally and externally.

TIP: If your dog doesn't like the taste or smell of coconut oil, you can try the REFINED coconut oil. It is said that it contains less MCT than unrefined but you will still benefit from it. They also make an MCT oil that can be added without taste. Giving both coconut oil and MCT oils can have huge benefits on cognitive dysfunction as well. Look for dark glass bottles in products that contain oils. Read label to make sure it is pure coconut oil. Some are mixed with other oils.

Water
Next we will look at your water. If you don't have a water filter, get one! It is a thousand times better having one. I can't say this enough. It is crucial to you and your dog's health. A Chlorine and Fluoride-free multi-stage filter or reverse osmosis and a fluoride filter added. You can get one pretty cheap. Check out my website for affordable water filters. I myself have one on my refrigerator for my water/ice dispenser (not the one that comes with the refrigerator inside) and one on my kitchen sink (under counter) as well as my shower. A whole house filter is ideal but much more costly. So for a fast solution, get one smaller for at least drinking and cooking water for a price as low as $100-$200.

Fluoride and Chlorine have been classified as a neurotoxin. Our waters are contaminated with pesticides and medications. These are not removed when treatment plants filter the waters. Some city waters are even in much worst shape depending on where you live. Test your water with affordable test kits ($40+) available in stores and online. Find what is in your water and make sure you pick a filter that removes high amounts of these toxins and chemicals. Chlorine and Fluoride are known to cause Hypothyroidism also.

Do not think your city water is safe. Our waters are **not** safe, even the cleanest isn't clean. Provide water (and food) in stainless steel, glass or high quality ceramic bowls. Keep the bowls clean, wash with soap and water daily and provide fresh filtered chemical free, chlorine and fluoride-free water to your pets.

Distilled water is not acceptable. Distilled water has had all the minerals removed. The body needs minerals. Filtered only! And make sure you add in minerals into the diet daily. You can do this easily using Fulvic/Humic Acid.

Tip: Cooking with fluoridated water simply concentrates fluoride in the food, a point that all pet food manufacturers must consider in addition to the ingredients they use in their manufactured pet foods.

Air
While the outside air may contain pollutants and do harm, inside your home make sure you have a good filtration system. Adding HEPA room air purifiers is a huge plus. Buy several and use in main rooms and bedrooms. You will probably need more than one in your home depending on size of rooms.

Vaccines
Reduce vaccines. Do not give yearly vaccines as they are not necessary. Do not give on the day of surgery or when your dog is ill. After getting puppy shots, you can do titer testing in the future. You may want to skip the Leptospirosis vaccine. Rabies is the only vaccine required by law so get with a vet that offers a Thimerosal-Free 3-year vaccine. This is a law in the USA although some towns will push the one-year. Check with your city ordinance and find a vet that offers the 3-year vaccine. According to whether you live in the country or city will determine what you may need to give for the other vaccines.

There are Rattlesnake vaccines, Flu vaccines; you name it. They are coming up with different vaccines on a daily basis for the pharmaceutical companies and vets to be able to make more money. And most of these do not work at all. Choose wisely and avoid vaccines if unnecessary or that don't really work like the flu vaccine.
Titering is always recommended so you don't subject your dog to more disease-causing vaccines. Distemper and Rabies given together have been known to cause aggression in dogs.
Flu vaccines will not keep your dog from getting the flu, just like human flu vaccines. They are also loaded with metals and toxins. Avoid! Bordetella is a vaccine I wouldn't recommend either. If you must, use the nasal or oral medication only. Do **not** use the injectable and don't give it on the same day as any other vaccine. For dogs less than 12 lbs, ask for only half the vaccine. You have to use the full Rabies vaccine due to laws but the others you should use only half or adjusted dosage for your size of dog. It also has been said that vaccines can be more harmful in white dogs.
Make sure your vet does not give one vaccine that is the combination of all. Each should be given in single doses and at least 2-4 weeks apart. I myself would wait a month in-between. This should apply to puppies and all dogs.

Vaccines are contaminated with mercury, aluminum, bacteria and who knows what else. Many of these ingredients are also categorized as a neurotoxin. Vaccines can cause other diseases such as arthritis, auto-immune disease, lameness, cancer, seizures and even death. It's best to avoid vaccines at all costs as much as possible. As for the Bordetella, you can treat kennel cough using natural remedies such as Mullein, Astragalus, and Echinacea. *See more at the end of this book.* Give a small dose of Zinc for 3-5 days before vaccines. Zinc in high doses is toxic to humans and pets. (For example: Normally a human dose is 30-40mg, give your dog 5-10mg) Extra Magnesium works well too. Magnesium Malate or Citrate is recommended.

You can add in vitamin C (Magnesium Ascorbate) to the diet. Adding in a little extra Selenium, Zinc, Curcumin and Quercetin are great as well. Try to give these within an hour of getting the vaccine. Astaxanthin is good at protecting against the toxic effects of the vaccine as well.

Lots of sunshine is needed as well for vitamin D.

Do not give your dog mushrooms, whey protein or beta-glucans during this process. Avoid all immune-stimulating supplements.

Avoid oils that suppress immunity and increase inflammation such as corn, safflower, sunflower, soybean, canola and peanut oils. Make sure your dog won't be under stress from travel (vacations) or guests in your home. Keep things calm and no stress for your dog for several weeks. You can also apply a cold pack to injection area as soon as you get home from getting vaccine. Do that a couple times during the day. It helps to block the immune reaction. It's best to do it immediately after vaccine if you want to carry an ice pack with you, otherwise do it ASAP. Maybe have one handy in your vehicle.

Core Vaccines
These are the only vaccines recommended:
- Rabies (Thimerosal-Free)
- Distemper
- Parvovirus

(For puppies its best to wait till 6 months of age for vaccines to reduce many unwanted reactions. This means keep your new dog inside and away from everyone and other animals and stay with your new pup at all times.)

Never get combo vaccines. Single dose only of each and wait 30 days in-between each. It is recommended to do titers for canine distemper and parvovirus every three years up until age 10. Seniors do not need any more vaccines due to age or if any dog has a chronic illness. This includes new injuries, any illness etc. Get a waiver if your dog has an illness or injury or wait until they are healthy and their immune system is strong again. It is stated by the manufacture of the vaccines to NOT give to an ill or diseased pet. Vaccines actually last 7-15 years but requesting titers will help you find if your dog is protected. Also note; studies on severe reactions have **not** been done on vaccines.

Best to avoid these vaccines:
Most of these don't protect or are not the right strains. Money makers for manufactures and vets.
Lyme (borelia)
Bordetella (kennel cough)
Parainfluenza (flu)
Leptospirosis
Adenovirus (hepatitis)
Rattlesnake
Coronavirus

Dr. Jean Dodds has a slightly different protocol for vaccines. She recommends core vaccines at an earlier age. But from what I have learned from human vaccines as well as pets, the longer you wait the less of a chance of reactions or lifetime side effects (Seizures, Autoimmune disorders, etc.) **Do not vaccinate your dog if it has had a serious life-threatening vaccine reaction.**

For Vaccine Reactions (to reduce or eliminate symptoms):
Use Thuja (200c preferably) for vaccines several days before, day of and several days after up to four weeks usually. Use Lyssin (200c preferably if found)-check Amazon or other websites) for Rabies vaccine for several days before, day of and after up to four weeks. You can use the 30c if you can't get your hands on the 200c.

If your dog is experiencing any symptoms of reactions from vaccines, continue the Lyssin and/or Thuja until symptoms are completely gone.

FOR DOGS 100 lbs TO 150 lbs: 5 pellets given at one time is one dose. Use one dose of 5 pellets daily for 3 days prior to rabies vaccination and continue on the day of vaccination and daily for one week following vaccination.

FOR DOGS 50 lbs up to 100 lbs: 4 pellets given at one time is one dose. Use one dose of 4 pellets daily for 3 days prior to rabies vaccination and continue on the day of vaccination and daily for one week following vaccination.

FOR DOGS 15 lbs up to 50 lbs: 3 pellets given at one time is one dose. Use one dose of 3 pellets daily for 3 days prior to Rabies vaccination and continue on the day of vaccination and daily for one week following vaccination.

FOR DOGS LESS THAN 15 lbs: 2 pellets given at one time are one dose. Use one dose of 2 pellets daily for 3 days prior to Rabies vaccination and continue on the day of vaccination and daily for one week following vaccination. Do not touch the pellets. You may put pellets in the mouth or put into a glass bottle, add filtered water, shake vigorously, let dissolve then squirt into your dog's mouth using a syringe or dropper. Keep refrigerated for up to two weeks. You can also add into food although there is much controversy but it has been noted by holistic Drs that it still works.

If your dog is still showing reactions to a vaccine, you can give this dose twice a day for several weeks up to a month or as long as needed until you see improvement. You may give pellets every 2 hours with bad reactions.

Medications
When your dog is sick, you take them to the vet and the vet writes a prescription and sends you home without any warning or warning label on these deadly medications and side effects. Depending on the illness, medications should be used only when absolutely necessary and sometimes shouldn't be used at all depending on the cause. There are many other options to use that do not include medications. Always check out the insert for warnings and contraindications. NSAIDs, steroids as well as flea and tick meds are highly dangerous and should be used with **extreme** caution and given only if absolutely necessary. There are dogs that die every day from using these medications. You can ask for Tramadol. Tramadol doesn't work against inflammation so adding in anti-inflammatory herbs would work with Tramadol. If you need pain meds longer than 2 weeks, I highly recommend you check out a supplement called CanineActiv. It may replace the pain meds completely depending on what you need pain meds for. Do not just jump on the band wagon and give medications prescribed by your vet until you do your research first. You may save your own dogs life.

Heartworm preventatives are not preventatives. You can give
Heartgard every 45 days which is by manufactures recommendations
although I wouldn't use these chemicals.
I myself live in the heart of mosquito country and it stays hot and
humid here about 8-9 months out of the year. And I do not give
heartworm preventatives that contain chemicals. I give once a week
the Heartworm nosode. I do have my dogs tested every 6 months to
make sure they are Heartworm negative. Nothing prevents heartworms. NOTHING! Most raw fed dogs have a smaller chance of infected mosquitoes biting them because raw fed dogs are healthier and
mosquitoes prey on weakened immune systems. Heartworm preventatives are not needed if the temperature drops below 57 degrees and
stays below that for at least 2 weeks. It kills off the mosquitoes. (Read
Chapter on Heartworms for more information)

Flea and tick products including topicals (store bought or from the
vet's office) are toxic and deadly and thousands of pets have died
from these topicals. They make plenty of natural products that work
just as well. Cedar oil works well. Use a carrier oil to dilute the cedar
oil and apply to the coat lightly.

Immune Systems
Immune systems are weakened when you use medications, vaccines,
poor diet, unfiltered water and chemical laced environmental
conditions. It is important to know when to use added supplements to
rebuild the system if these conditions occur. A strong immune system
will ward off fleas, ticks, mosquitoes and most of all, diseases. It is
vital that you keep your dog's immune system strong by doing all the
things mentioned here.

Disease
Poor diet, vaccines, medications, unfiltered water, the air we breathe
and the ground we walk on is laced with pesticides and chemicals that
are deadly to us and our pets. We have higher cancer rates in the USA
than we did 20-30 years ago. More preservatives and additives have
been added to our foods and waters. This includes our lawn fertilizers
and medications. We must avoid all of these as much as possible. It is
a critical time for all of us. Cancer, heart conditions, Diabetes, Cush-
ing's, autoimmune disease, arthritis/lameness, and seizures/epilepsy

just to name a few of what these toxins do to our bodies. Use organic all-natural fertilizers on your yard and pesticides that are not harmful to children or pets if you must use anything. Food Grade Diatomaceous Earth works for many things. Kills insects, fleas, great for cleaning, deworming, cleansing the body, added benefits for arthritis and over-all health. Too many to list here. Sprinkle it all over your yard and add into your dog's food. Pumpkin seeds or organic pumpkin seed powder kills all parasites except heartworms.

Vet Visits
Vet visits should consist of wellness visits every 6 months for a senior or diseased dog and once a year for healthy dogs. Complete blood workup including checking calcium levels (I always check for these things along with any deficiencies that may show up with supplements), Heartworm test, thyroid test, x-rays if needed in an aging dog or a dog prone to hip dysplasia or joint issues. Run a ProBNP blood test to check for early heart disease. If your dog shows early signs, get them on D-Ribose, Hawthorn, Dandelion Leaf, Taurine and COQ10. Depending on your breed of dog and what they may be predisposed to, run tests for those genetic diseases as well as often as necessary. Veterinarian visits should not be determined by what your vet says is a must. If your vet tries to put your dog on a prescription pet food diet, refuse. You have other options. That is horrible food and actually makes things worse. Organic boiled chicken, organic scrambled eggs and a little added organic 100% pumpkin to the diet is always acceptable on a short-term for digestive problems like diarrhea and vomiting. Don't forget your organic bone broth. Refuse vaccines and receive only if needed on your terms. Do your research. Speaking of doing your research, don't go to one website and believe what you read. Go to several ones that don't have the exact same wording. Find reputable websites you can trust.
Many pet owners who have made the switch to raw or a homemade diet have noticed drastic changes in their pets, including:

- Shinier, healthier skin and coats
- Cleaner teeth
- Improved digestion
- Improvement with allergy symptoms

- Anal gland problems cleared up
- Decreased shedding
- Firmer, smaller stools

This is a basic guide for raw diets. It's simple and it can be cheaper than any premium type pet food out there. Your vet bills will decrease. It will be best to do your yearly blood work. Yearly checkups are important. Every 6 months for seniors.
B-Complex, Magnesium, and Manganese vitamins are a great addition to the diet and will help joints as well (Pitties/Staffies) and large dogs need these always as they are more apt for an ACL tear and other joint issues). If you want in-depth testing for allergies, vitamins or alike, there are several experts out there that offer this. Dr. Peter Dobias offers hair testing for minerals and toxins and Dr. Jean Dodds offers blood work for thyroid and food sensitivities.

Kefir and yogurt (plain organic) is good for an added probiotic but it isn't enough so you will need to add in a probiotic supplement. Raw goat's milk is a great immune builder as well.

After 6 months on a raw diet and you have been using the recommended supplements here, you can reduce the amount of some of these supplements if your dog isn't having any skin or allergy issues. I sometimes give every other day except for fish oils and joint supplements. I give those daily unless I am feeding sardines too.
Continue the vitamin E three times a week. If you miss a dose of these on any given day, don't panic. It takes awhile before the dog will start to show deficiencies and you would have to miss quite a few days. I also will skip at least one day on supplements per week except the joint supplements. You can also switch to a different brand. It's best to rotate brands so find some really good ones and rotate them about every 3-6 months or so.
Joint supplements should be given to all dogs of all ages starting at about 6-12 months of age. This will help to prevent future arthritis, hip dysplasia etc. More about joints later. The bigger the dog, the sooner to start them.

Tips:
Dogs prone to digestive upsets or vomiting immediately following a meal will benefit from using a bowl for fast eaters. These dogs will definitely need to start on digestive enzymes and probiotics weeks before transitioning. I also like to add in a digestive enzymes with ox bile or something specific for pancreas as this helps with stomach issues as well. Also try the ground-up meats instead so they can't gulp chunks and get food stuck in their throat.

If your dog is experiencing runny/loose stools (soft stool is not diarrhea), constipation or vomiting at times other than after meals, slow down the transition process and add 100% organic pumpkin (canned is ok) to their meal. Use 1-2 tablespoons per cup of food. Pumpkin is unique in that it helps with loose stools as well as constipation and upset tummies. Slippery Elm is great for digestive issues and leaky gut. If you are adding organ meat in the beginning stop these for a few days or until the system has adjusted to the change then slowly add back in using small amounts at a time. If these suggestions don't work, try fasting your dog for 24 hours. Let the digestive system rest. Feed smaller meals and more often. Start back with bone broth.

Dogs with allergies/food intolerances, find a protein in the exotics to start with. Rabbit or goat is good. Exotic meats are higher in price so look for deals.

Dogs that have been on steroids, antibiotics, or other long-term drugs, may experience longer detoxification periods. You should always consult with a holistic veterinarian if you believe your dog is showing severe problems associated with the diet change. You can always start off cooking or searing the meats to avoid these types of reactions.

It is important to remember, never feed your dog one hour before and one hour after exercise, this will prevent bloat and life-threatening gastric torsion especially in larger dogs.

Transitioning Picky Eaters and Older Dogs to a Raw Diet
These dogs may turn their noses up at the smell and texture of their new food. Don't worry, as this is a common occurrence (particularly with smaller dogs) and is usually easy to address by following these steps:
- Eliminate treats during the transition

- Fast your dog the night before starting the transition
- Partially cook/sear the meats
- Add cooked shredded chicken on top along with broth
- Add low sodium sardines in with the food

FYI - Most vets are unfamiliar with raw diets and do not support them due to their lack of knowledge and education in nutrition. Don't let your vet discourage you and if you get repeated lashings so to speak from your vet, FIND A NEW ONE! It's YOUR dog and YOUR money. You have the final say.

Once you have transitioned and all is going well, you can always do a full body cleanse. This is optional but you may give it a try if your dog had shown a lot of signs of detoxing throughout the diet transition. He/she may need a deeper cleanse. Your dog may also suffer from leaky gut. That's a dog that no matter what you try or do, the issues are still there. Like allergy symptoms or stomach and digestive issues, eye discharge, itchy ears etc.

Deeper cleansing may consist of Activated Charcoal, Milk Thistle, Burdock Root, Dandelion, Apple Cider Vinegar and/or Colloidal Silver. Many things will cleanse the body. Even organic mushroom blends.
Since you have already added in the greens powder by this time, you can add in Rose hips. It is a diuretic and it is great for many things including joints. It contains high amounts of vitamin C. It is a great "go to" for adding vitamin C in a natural form to the diet. Much healthier than synthetic vitamin C supplements. After a couple of weeks, you can add in the Milk Thistle. You don't want to add in supplements all at once. Meaning don't start all new ones on the same day. Give it 3-5 days at least in-between each. Two at a time is a safe start. You may get some opposite reactions like rapid detox or digestive upset, which you don't want if you throw them all in at once. You want it to go slowly but you want to cleanse the entire body. And start with a smaller amount and work up to the recommended amount.

If your dog is ill or has a weakened immune system, try organic bone broth

It is great for an ill dog or one that needs a boost in their immune system, that doesn't want to eat, and/or has some aches and pains. This is high in Glucosamine so this will give a boost as well. Also try feeding organic/pasture-fed scrambled eggs and some organic/pasture-fed cooked chicken breast meat. It's like when we get sick; we reach for the chicken soup. Bone Broth works the same way. It is a great soup for adding electrolytes back into the body as well.

Bone Broth

To make it, you will need:
- Organic Chicken with bone
- Raw unfiltered Apple Cider Vinegar with "mother"
- Filtered water (Chlorine and fluoride-free)

How I make it is I put a whole chicken into the crock-pot. I pour in at least 1 tablespoon of Apple Cider Vinegar per gallon of water. It helps break the bones down and you may need to add more during the cooking process. Let it cook. This may take 24-48 hours. Check it occasionally.

You can feed the cooked chicken (not the bones) once it falls off the bone. Continue cooking bones until you can mash them with a fork. You can strain out the bigger pieces and feed the broth to your pets. Yum! Good for you too!

Additional Nutritional Foods in Powder Form

These can be added if you choose for added nutrition. These help build the immune system, add in many minerals, vitamins, amino acids and help build the immune system. It's a great way to alternate or add in on occasion or pick a mix of them and add into diet at anytime for added nutrients. Most fight cancer and are immune builders. Make sure they are not from China or India. It's much better than giving a multi-vitamin supplement made from synthetic vitamins. You can use the ones listed below if you aren't adding in any fruits in raw form to the diet. It's a great substitute.

These include:
Organic Goji Berry Powder
Enhances the immune system, protects eyesight and supports the liver. High in vitamin C and A. Found on many sites including nuts.com, Amazon etc.

Organic Blueberry Powder
Such a wonderful fruit to add. It is an antioxidant. Great for heart disease, cancer, weakened immune systems, osteoporosis, memory loss, bladder infections and so much more. Full of fiber as well. Found on nuts.com. Easy to find anywhere in an organic form.

Organic Red/Black Raspberry Powder
Raspberries rank near the top of all fruits for antioxidant strength, due to their rich content of ellagic acid, quercetin, gallic acid, anthocyanins, cyanidins, pelargonidins, catechins, kaempferol and salicylic acid. Raspberries possess almost 50% higher antioxidant activity than strawberries, and three times that of kiwis. Znaturalfoods.com sells an organic red raspberry powder.

Organic Bitter Melon Extract
Shown multiple actions against pancreatic cancer cells. Helps to regulate blood glucose levels. It may help to maintain the body's defense mechanism in weather changes or air borne pathogen. Rich in iron and has twice the beta carotene of broccoli. Has a bitter taste. Starwest Botanicals makes an organic form but found on many websites.

Organic Mangosteen Fruit Rind
The nutritional benefits of the mangosteen fruit are found in the **peel/rind,** which contains high levels of xanthanoids and other phyto-chemicals with strong antioxidant properties. Znaturalfoods.com sells an organic powder.

Organic Grape Seed Extract Powder
When purchasing grape seed extract supplements, make VERY certain that all ingredients including inactive ingredients do not contain grape skins or the meat of grapes. ONLY SEEDS. The seeds are very powerful and are considered a powerful antioxidant. Great for in-

flammation as well. Kills cancer cells. I found Organic Grape Seed Extract Powder called Biofinest Grape seed Extract Powder. It's 100% grape **seeds** and organic.

Organic Cranberry Powder
Cranberries are known for their use in the healing and prevention of urinary tract infections. Regular consumption has shown that cranberries can help boost memory, relieve stress, anxiety or depression and can help promote weight gain. Cranberries can help prevent cancer cells from multiplying or developing. Most all cranberry comes from the USA. Found all over in organic powder form but frozen can work as well. Blend them up and serve.

Organic Acai Berry Powder
Acai Berry is loaded with antioxidants, a combination of essential amino acids and is packed with monounsaturated and polyunsaturated fatty acids (omega-6 & omega-9). This berry is said to contain more antioxidants than blueberries, cranberries and strawberries. Found at various websites including Amazon.

You may also look for frozen organic fruit to blend or feed as well. Frozen organic foods are just as good as these powders if not better. Stay away from the 'spray freeze' method. This method uses high heat processing. You want freeze-dried or micro-dried in powder or frozen organic in stores.

Taurine
If you are cooking your dog's meats, you should add Taurine into the diet. *Taurine is found in raw heart muscle.*
Taurine is best given on an empty stomach. Note that Taurine is abundant in raw meat, particularly heart, but much is lost when the meat is cooked. Cooking reduces Taurine, so feed raw or cook lightly. Vitamin B6 is needed for the conversion of Taurine, so add a B-complex vitamin supplement as well if needed.

Dosage:
Small dog: Up to 250mg
Medium dog: Up to 500mg
Large dog: Up to 750mg

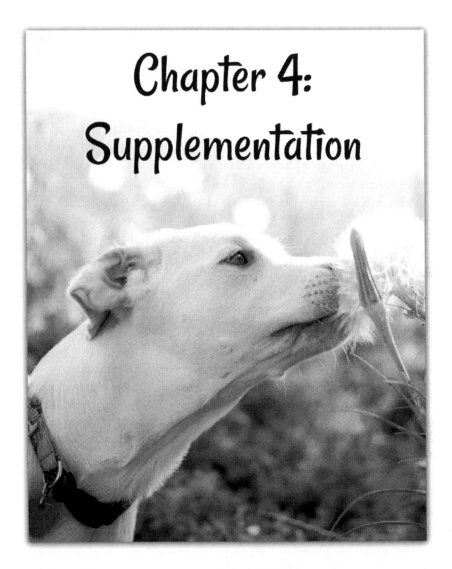

Chapter 4:
Supplementation

Chapter 4
Supplementation

Curcumin/Turmeric (optional): Turmeric (Curcumin or Kurkuma) should not be confused with "turmeric root," a colloquial name for the plant commonly known as Goldenseal (*Hydrastis canadensis*), which is in the *Ranunculaceae*, or buttercup family and is a popular herbal remedy in its own right. Goldenseal can be toxic if overused, whereas few adverse effects have been recorded regarding the frequent consumption of Turmeric. Turmeric or Curcumin works well for all types of illnesses. Cancer, Arthritis, weakened immune systems. When supplementing using this, add in black pepper and coconut oil to enhance its effects.

Turmeric should not be given to dogs prone to kidney stones. Turmeric isn't supposed to be given with blood thinners. Turmeric should not be combined with drugs that reduce stomach acid (Pepsid, Zantac etc), as the body will actually increase its production of stomach acid, and thus, lead to nausea, stomach pain, bloating, and esophagus damage.
Please ask your holistic vet if it is ok for your pet.

You can also make a Turmeric paste.

For paste:
1/2 cup organic Turmeric powder
1 1/2 cups or so of filtered water
1-1/2 teaspoon freshly ground organic black pepper
1/4 cup of organic unrefined virgin coconut oil

Heat water on low in pan, add Turmeric in. Stir until it has thickened up. Add pepper and coconut oil in. Remove from heat and let stand until it cools. Place into a clean glass container then refrigerate. You can store in refrigerator for up to about 2 weeks. You can add into your dog's food or into a liquidy food like kefir or cottage cheese. Start with a small amount. 1/4 teaspoon per 10 lbs is a good place to start then gradually work up if needed. Sometimes Turmeric can cause stomach upset so watch for loss of appetite.

Avoid Turmeric, Ginger and Garlic from countries such as China and India. That includes organic as well.

Digestive Enzymes (needed):
What happens when enzymes are depleted? When there are insufficient food enzymes for dogs, the full digestive burden will be placed on the dog's pancreas to produce digestive enzymes. An over-stressed digestive system can eventually lead to improper food digestion and nutrient malabsorption.

Signs of lacking in enzymes:
- Bloating
- Gas and/or diarrhea
- Bad breath
- Body odor
- Acid Reflux/GERD
- Sensitive tummies
- Allergies
- Skin issues
- Coprophagia (eating poop)
- Yeast infections
- Thyroid issues
- Leaky Gut

A lack of digestive enzymes is a major contributing factor at the root of cancer.

I have found some pretty good human digestive enzymes that I am using just for these issues listed above. For a dog with stomach issues, you may need a very high amount of enzymes with added probiotics along with something good for the pancreas such as ox bile.

Probiotics (needed):
Probiotics are most likely to be helpful in resolving or preventing canine diarrhea associated with diet, medication, stress, certain GI infections, inflammatory bowel disease, intestinal bacterial overgrowth and malabsorption. Replaces bad bacteria in the body with good bacteria. Builds a stronger immune system. Using probiotics and digestive enzymes help keep the immune system strong and the digestive tract functioning like a well oiled machine.

FYI - you cannot get enough of probiotics from dairy. You will need to use supplements to get the full benefits.

Slippery Elm (optional):
Slippery Elm can also be used in the same way as Milk Thistle except it works for dogs with sensitive digestive tracts. Slippery Elm is thought to soothe the bladder lining. Slippery Elm is high in Magne-

sium as well. It's also known to work well as a poultice for insect bites, scrapes etc. You can make a paste and apply to skin. It can be left on the spot for hours without harm. Make sure your dog gets plenty of water or moisture content when giving this. Use Slippery Elm for leaky gut and digestive issues.

Dosing is 1/4 teaspoon for every 10 lbs.

Slippery Elm should not be taken together with any medications as it may interfere with their absorption. Do not use this long term. Use for up to 3 months then stop. Wait several months and you can use it again if needed.

Fish oils (needed):
Always buy high quality fish oils. You will find many oils out there but not of good quality and therefore are rancid or loaded with Mercury. Follow dosing on bottle. Buy in glass or metal containers. NO plastic due to BPA and BPS (when it says BPA free, it usually contains BPS). The smaller the fish, the less mercury exposure. Also Calamari oil is a great oil as well as Green Lipped Mussel. Krill oil is **not** recommended due to the over fishing of krill and the decline of krill in oceans.

Stop fish oil and Vitamin E seven days before surgery.

The areas with the highest contamination levels include most of the Atlantic Ocean, the Gulf of Mexico, the Chesapeake Bay, the waters around Northern Europe and China. These are areas that have been industrialized for many years.
The waters surrounding New Zealand are some of the cleanest on the planet. Industrialization is mostly limited to the North Island. The waters are far away from major shipping lanes. The government has many regulations in place that help to protect the environment, prevent pollution and ensure that the fish populations are sustainable.

Follow label or...
Daily Dose:
Small dogs (up to 30 lbs): 250 - 500mg
Medium dogs (31-50 lbs): 750 - 1000mg

Large dogs (51-80 lbs): 125 - 1500mg
Giant dogs (81+ lbs): 1700 - 2000mg

Vitamin E (needed 3 times a week): Vitamin E is a powerful antioxidant that plays a crucial role in supporting pet health. Pet food alone does not contain enough vitamin E to meet your dog's needs. Supplementing your dog's diet with natural vitamin E can help prevent serious health problems created by vitamin E deficiency. It is a must especially when giving fish oils. Most of your vitamin E supplements contain soy. Avoid soy in all products. Do not give softgels to dogs. They go in one end and out the other without dissolving. Soy free recommendations can be found on website as I am constantly updating as they are found.

Dosage:
Small dogs - 200IU
Med/Large - 300-400IU
Giant - 600IU

A diet high in carbohydrates can also deplete vitamin E.

Stop Vitamin E seven days before surgery.

Natural vitamin E is known as "**d**-alpha-tocopherol." This is the most biologically active form of vitamin E.
Synthetic vitamin E is known as "**dl**-alpha-tocopherol." You need "approximately 50% more IU of synthetic alpha tocopherol" to get the same nutritional effect.

Vitamin C (recommended but can be found in Rosehips, Camu Camu and Amla): Vitamin C is highly recommended especially in healing any pets with a disease or illness. Give high amounts for illness until bowel tolerance. Synthetic vitamin C is still absorbed in smaller amounts and can still be beneficial to your dog, especially a sick dog. Ascorbic Acid is hard on the stomach so you should provide a buffered vitamin C, which is Sodium Ascorbate, Calcium Ascorbate or Magnesium Ascorbate. Sodium Ascorbate contains sodium so our dogs don't really need that. Calcium Ascorbate contains calcium so if you are already giving calcium, more isn't needed. So I recommend

Magnesium Ascorbate due to **all** diets lacking in Magnesium. I like to recommend a natural form of vitamin C. Rosehips and Camu Camu along with Amla have the highest vitamin C content. Camu Camu has the very highest. Buffered vitamin C supplements are synthetic; the body will accept some of it but a lot of it is wasted in the body. You really have to give high amounts to get the best benefits. Always use caution when giving higher amounts; give to bowel tolerance then back off slightly. This is good in higher amounts for ill dogs or seniors. If you use the whole food forms, your side effects will be much less if any at all.

Dosage:
Adjust accordingly but a good place to start or work towards.
Small dogs: 500mg - 1500mg
Medium/Large dogs: 1000mg - 3000mg
Giant dogs: 2000mg - 4000mg

WARNING: Avoid anything with Benzene, Benzoate, or Benzoic Acid; especially when combined with Ascorbic Acid, Citric Acid, and vitamin C ingredients. ***It becomes a toxic carcinogen.***

Rosehips: Dogs can greatly benefit from Rosehips as well. Rosehips are a great additional supplement for treating and preventing arthritis and many other diseases. It has a high amount of vitamin C. It has a tart flavor but dogs don't seem to mind it. It's less expensive than Camu Camu. Camu Camu has one of the highest concentrations of vitamin C of any food source. Camu Camu has 200 times more vitamin C than a banana in terms of vitamin C per ounce.

Dosage:
Small dogs: 1/4-1/2 teaspoon daily
Med. Dogs: 1/2-1 teaspoon
Large dogs: 1-2 teaspoon

Magnesium (needed): Dogs need to have Magnesium in their diet. Even with the best diet, your dog will probably be deficient. And if your dog is prone to ACL injuries, this is a **requirement** in the diet. Without the right level of magnesium, unabsorbed calcium can build up in your dog's body causing Arthritis.

If you would like to add a Magnesium supplement to your dog's diet or your own:

Magnesium Citrate can be used for oxalate stones (can have laxative effect)
Magnesium Taurate for low stomach acid (calming, for heart, can make blood sugar fluctuate)
Magnesium Glycinate (no laxative effect, high absorption, for muscle pain, calming)
Magnesium Malate (for achy joints and/or muscles, for heart, can cause stomach upset, no laxative effect)
Magnesium Orotate (for heart, high absorbing magnesium)
Magnesium L-Threonate (for brain, absorbs well, calming, no laxative effect)
Magnesium Aspartate (for fatigue and muscle)
Magnesium Chloride (for cellular detoxification and tissue purification)
Magnesium Lactate (for moderate absorption, avoid with kidney issues).

**Magnesium Stearate, Magnesium Gluconate and Magnesium Oxide should be avoided.

Dosage:
Small dogs: 10mg - 20mg
Medium dogs: 20mg - 50mg
Large dogs: 50mg - 75mg
Giant dogs: 75mg - 100mg
Or when using powder 1/4 teaspoon up to 1/2 teaspoon depending on size of dog.

Ubiquinol/COQ10 (optional): As your dog reaches middle age, his level of CoQ10 gradually diminishes. You may be wondering if your dog can get CoQ10 from his/her diet. Food sources of CoQ10 include oily fish like mackerel, salmon, and sardines, organ meats and whole grains. If your pet were to consume a diet high in these sources every day, they would still be faced with their body's decreased ability to convert CoQ10 into the active form that they need as they age. This helps with many ailments such as heart disease, blood sugar and joints as well. Your dog's body requires this essential coenzyme to function properly. Your dog can benefit from an extra dose of Ubiquinol or COQ10 especially in older dogs. Ubiquinol absorbs more easily so more effective and less needed.

Ubiquinol Dosage:
Small dogs: 50mg per day
Medium dogs: 100mg per day
Large dogs: 100mg twice per day
Giant dogs: 100-200mg twice per day

COQ10 Dosage:
Small dogs: 100 - 200mg daily
Medium dogs: 200 - 300mg daily
Large dogs: 300 - 400mg daily
Giant dogs: 400 - 500mg daily

Colostrum (optional): If you are giving your dog a Glucosamine supplement, add pasture-fed Colostrum to help the body to absorb the Glucosamine better. It helps to build immunity for a weakened immune system.

Colostrum from pasture-fed cows is much higher in immune factors than a human mother's colostrum! It's the immune boosting properties that make colostrum an important supplement. Researchers have shown that colostrum is one of the most important nutritional supplements available for enhancing the immune system and helping in tissue repair. Colostrum works well for dogs and cats with diarrhea and for weakened immune systems. Colostrum can be used in all animals and humans. Colostrum is known for healing and sealing the gut. A great addition for leaky gut. It takes approximately 6 weeks to heal a leaky gut using Colostrum, sometimes longer.

Lactoferrin is another component of colostrum, which inhibits the growth of pathogenic organisms. Colostrum shows that it can be used to treat allergies, cancer, diarrhea, poor wound healing, hepatitis C, bacterial and viral infections, multiple sclerosis, obesity and peptic ulcers. Colostrum is useful in the treatment of ulcerative colitis, inflammatory bowel disease and chemotherapy-induced mucositis. It's best if given at least 30 minutes before feeding time. The organic grass-fed is rather expensive but worth it for really sick animals. They also make a colostrum called Colostrum LD. It is liposomal Colostrum, meaning Liposomal Delivery (LD) system is an applied coating which allows colostrum to dissolve in liquids and ensures the colostrum will bypass digestion and will be transported through the bowel wall; circulate throughout the body and will reach the organs and cells to remain bioavailable at the cellular level. It comes from pasture-fed cows.

Dosage:
1/2 tsp per 25 pounds of body weight once per day.
You may notice changes as soon as one day to 2 months.

Calcium (needed): One of the most common mistakes that people make when feeding a home-cooked diet is not adding in Calcium. You **must** add Calcium when you feed a diet that does not include bones. Adult dogs need around 800 to 1,000 mg of Calcium per pound of food fed.

The ideal Calcium: Phosphorus ratio in the canine diet is between 1:1 and 2:1. Meat contains a lot of Phosphorus, so the more meat a diet contains, the more Calcium will be required to reach the correct Calcium: Phosphorus ratio. Adding 800 to 1,000 mg of Calcium will provide the correct Calcium: Phosphorus ratio even for a high-meat diet, unless you use a Calcium supplement that also contains Phosphorus. In that case, moderately higher amounts of Calcium may be needed to balance out the additional Phosphorus contained in the supplement.

Ground eggshell can be used as a Calcium supplement. Rinse eggshells and dry them on a counter overnight, or in the oven, then grind them in a clean coffee grinder. One large eggshell provides one teaspoon of ground eggshell, which contains 2,000 mg of Calcium, so add 1/2-teaspoon ground eggshell per pound of food fed. Don't use eggshells that haven't been ground to powder, as they may not be absorbed as well.

I recommend powdered Calcium you can use in place of above. A powdered seaweed Calcium or a powdered eggshell Calcium will work well adding into wet foods.

Bone meal is **not** recommended. Bone meal is sourced from other countries in most all cases. High heat processing is usually done by manufactures making it harder for your dog to digest. Bone meal may also contain high amounts of Fluoride and Lead and is no longer a recommended source of calcium for humans or pets. Bone meal in pet foods is 10 times more contaminated.

Milk Thistle (needed certain times): Milk Thistle contains a flavonoid compound called "Silymarin" which itself is a combination of several other active compounds.
Milk Thistle should only be used as a medicinal herb for the treatment of liver disorders and other health problems or for an occasional detox. Not to be used long-term in healthy dogs. Use for detoxing every 6 months after initial detox for up to 30 days.

The standard dosage of Milk Thistle extract is based on a Silymarin content of around 80 percent. Most supplements of Milk Thistle contain about 100 to 200 mg of the herb.
For dogs with advanced liver disease, a dosage as high as 200 mg per 10 pounds of body weight is possible. For other liver problems or health conditions, 75 to 100 mg per 10 pounds of body weight per day is sufficient to see results.

If Milk Thistle causes upset stomach, gas, or mild diarrhea in your dogs, simply reduce the dosage.

If your dog is coming off of commercial pet foods, drinks unfiltered water, takes medications, gets vaccines often, has liver issues or in his senior years you can give this for 3-6 months then remove from the diet. It shouldn't be given permanently to healthy pets but can be given off and on throughout. Always remember, anytime you are giving herbs, take 1-2 days off a week from giving these. The body needs to clear out the build up and not become immune to anything it is getting in a vitamin or supplement form. Under certain cases such as moderate to severe joint issues you should not stop joint supplements and possibly other supplements depending on the dog and its medical background. Each case will be different.

Coconut oil - organic unrefined virgin (recommended): Coconut oil aids allergies, skin issues such as dry skin and hair, ear infections, yeast buildup, healing wounds or sores. (Trader Joe's carries a good one in a glass jar as well as Kroger's Brand (Simple Truth-organic.) Look for glass jars. Remember, plastic contains BPA like cans. Coconut oil is considered an antibacterial, antiviral and anti-fungal agent. It's also considered a healthy fat.

Dose: 1/4-1/2 teaspoon per 10 lbs.

Start with smaller amounts and work up to recommended dosage. I myself give it every other day and sometimes about 3 times a week. Depends on how much your dog needs it but you cannot go wrong with daily feeding.

ACV (Raw, Organic and with "Mother") (recommended): Apple Cider Vinegar has excellent antibacterial and antifungal properties.

Internal use: Apple Cider Vinegar is good in maintaining the acid/alkaline balance of the digestive tract. ACV works well for all types of problems. Indigestion, allergies, yeast buildup, arthritis, recurrent UTI's, Cancer and prevention of bladder and kidney stones.

Dosage:
0-25 lbs: 1 teaspoon
25-50 lbs: 2 teaspoons
50-75 lbs: 1 TBSP
75+ lbs: 1 1/2-2 TBSP

External use: It is effective at fighting itching and scratching from allergies or bites. When applied directly to a hot spot on your dog's skin, ACV will calm the redness and swelling all while providing your dog with some much needed relief. ACV can be poured directly on your dog's fur after a bath and then rinsed, which will cure dandruff, rejuvenate hair and help balance the PH levels in the body. White vinegar is not recommended for use.

71

Humic/Fulvic Acid (Minerals) (recommended):
Many pet parents wonder if their dogs will be getting "too many minerals" if they are giving other products that also contain minerals such as a Calcium supplement. The answer is no because Fulvic is extracted from plant material – not rocks or clay. Humic/Fulvic acid contains over 90 minerals, amino acids and several vitamins. When plant-derived Fulvic enters the system, it is immediately recognized as one of nature's essential substances. It triggers the proper metabolic responses that utilize the minerals where they're needed, discarding those that are not needed. It is impossible for plant-derived minerals to build up in the tissues. Depending on the severity of health issues, you can double the amount. Fulvic/Humic Acid detoxifies the body of heavy metals, toxins, and pollutants, increases oxygen absorption in blood, enhances healing, repair, and rejuvenation of the cells - energizes cells, repairs and detoxifies the thyroid. It can help decrease digestive issues such as SIBO symptoms (small intestine bacterial overgrowth), inflammatory bowel disorders, leaky gut, bacterial infections like respiratory and urinary tract infections or the flu and common colds. It's an all-natural plant form. It helps boost absorption of nutrients.

Do not give alongside medications. Wait 2 hours in-between. While overdosing is impossible, in higher amounts there can be nausea and diarrhea, similar to taking high amounts of vitamin C.

Dosage:
Small dogs: 1 teaspoon
Medium dogs: 2 teaspoons
Large dogs: 1 TBSP

B Vitamins (recommended):
The B-complex vitamins help ward off stress, alleviate neurological problems, and are essential for cell maintenance and growth, the production of antibodies and red blood cells, and the absorption of protein, fat, and carbohydrates.

The B-complex vitamins are grouped together because they work as a team. The team is made up of Thiamine (B1), Riboflavin (B2), Niacin (B3), Pantothenic Acid (B5), Pyridoxine (B6), **Methyl**cobalamin

(B12), Biotin, **Folate** and Choline. The effectiveness of one B vitamin is to a large extent dependent upon adequate amounts of other B vitamins. For example, Pyridoxine (B6) is necessary for the absorption of **Methyl**cobalamin (B12). Natural food sources rich in B vitamins never contain only one B vitamin. It is best to supplement the B vitamins together. You can give your dog extra B-complex supplement when you know it is going to be stressed or the immune system is compromised. Vaccinations, surgery, traveling, separation anxiety and/or serious injury or shock to the body are the most extreme cases in which your dog's body needs a lot of extra support from the B vitamins. The B-complex vitamins will also reduce the toxic effects of antibodies and radiation from x-rays or radiation therapy.

*Make sure the B-12 form is **Methyl**cobalamin and **not** **Cyano**cobalamin.*

*Folic acid is a synthetic. Look for **Folate**. Folic Acid causes cancer.*

Vitamins D, E, K, and A (DEKA) are fat-soluble.
Fat-soluble vitamins: Meaning they are stored in the liver. These should not be used in higher amounts unless recommended and supervised by your holistic vet or nutritionist.

For those who do not wish to feed raw liver, here are the dosages of vitamin A. Do not go over the dosage amounts. You can also try a liver powder from a good source to add into diet. Grass fed and/or organic preferably.

VITAMIN A (optional):
Dosage - once a day:
1,000 units per cup of food
OR:
Small dogs: 1,500 IU
Medium dogs: 3,750 IU
Large /Giant dogs: 5,000 IU

Pumpkin Seeds/ Powder (raw organic) (optional):
Pumpkin seeds contain the amino acid Cucurbitin, which paralyzes and helps eliminate worms from the digestive tract. A safe and natural

dewormer. Studies have shown that adding pumpkin seeds to the daily diet helps reduce inflammatory response due to conditions like arthritis, and helps prevent calcium **oxalate** stone formation. You can find them on numerous websites. Pumpkin seeds contain magnesium as well.

Astragalus *(Astragalus membranaceous)* **(optional):**
A great immune booster and even kill's cancer cells. Astragalus is a viable option for early treatment of various forms of respiratory infection, including kennel cough. Helps with anemia as well. Immunostimulant, antiviral, anti-inflammatory, hypothyroid (mildly depresses thyroid function), hypotensive, digestive tonic. Works on immune systems, lungs, liver, heart, kidneys, thyroid, and digestive tract.

Astragalus is used for strengthening the body against viral infections of the respiratory and heart. Astragalus can be used for early treatment of a variety of respiratory infections, including kennel cough (Bordetella bronchiseptica). Astragalus helps to raise white blood cell counts and also boosts the body's immune system. Astragalus may be useful for helping the body protect itself and speed recovery from the damages of long term steroid medications. Astragalus is also useful in early stages of kidney infection and/or renal failure. Astragalus is non-toxic in any dosages.
Astragalus may help prevent the immunosuppression caused by chemotherapy agents. In addition, it has been found that Astragalus contains an alkaloid that inhibits the spread of melanoma, a skin cancer.

Preservative-Free Joint Supplement - (Recommended):
(6 months or older for ALL dogs) Read Chapter on **Canine Arthritis and Joint Pain**

Greens Powders-(*Starwest Botanicals***) (if not adding in veggies):**
Ingredients: Organic Barley grass, organic Wheat grass, organic Spirulina, organic Spinach, organic Alfalfa leaf, organic Kelp, organic Dulse leaf, organic Orange peel, organic Barley grass juice, organic Beet root, organic Dandelion leaf, organic Lemon peel, organic Ginkgo leaf and organic Wheat grass juice.

For Greens Powder, you can reduce the amount to half or give every other day if dog is healthy and has not been ill or had any medications, vaccines, unfiltered water etc.

Dosage:
Small dogs: 1/4-1/2 teaspoon
Medium/Large dogs: 1/2-1 teaspoon
Giant dogs: 1-1 1/2 teaspoons

Greens contain some of your highest amount of vitamins. In today's world even the best-grown organic veggies and fruits are lacking in higher content of vitamins and minerals due to our depleted soils. Same for our meats. In a perfect world we wouldn't need extra supplementation but because of our meats lacking due to over-use of antibiotics and medications and poor diets fed to the cows and chickens and other animals we consume, we must add extra food sources. Although dogs are carnivores, giving a small amount of veggies or greens powder can have huge benefits for your dog due to what is lacking in our foods. Greens have your best sources for vitamins.

ORGANIC BARLEY GRASS: Over a dozen studies in several universities show the extract of young Barley leaves to be a useful and powerful therapeutic agent. Rich in SOD, Calcium, Iron and trace minerals. Barley has been reported to relieve arthritis, gastrointestinal disorders, chronic fatigue, constipation, poor circulation, and Psoriasis, Acne and body odor.

ORGANIC WHEAT GRASS: Well-known super-star among grasses. Wheat grass is rich in Choline and Chlorophyll. It has good amounts of vitamin A, C and E with small amounts of Thiamine, Riboflavin, Niacin, Pantothenic Acid and vitamin B6 and B12. Wheat grass is rich in Potassium and Phosphorus. It has good amounts of Calcium, Sodium and Magnesium with small amounts of Iron, Folic Acid, Selenium and Zinc.

ORGANIC SPIRULINA: Is a complete, highly digestible protein that is rich in B vitamins, particularly B-1, B-2, B-3, and B-6. Spirulina is the richest source of vitamin B-12 found in nature! Spirulina has also shown promise in the treatment of impaired immunity, protein deficiencies and eating disorders.

ORGANIC SPINACH: An excellent source of minerals like Calcium, Phosphorus, Iron, Potassium and Zinc as well as antioxidants like Carotenoids, vitamin C and vitamin E.

If your pet has had oxalate stones previously, do not give spinach to them. It does have a tendency to cause oxalate stones in some.

ORGANIC ALFALFA: The father of all foods, Alfalfa has roots that reach up to 60 feet into the soil to absorb trace minerals. Its lightweight proteins stimulate the rebuilding of tissues and strengthen hair, skin and nails. Also good for digestive system support and to stimulate the appetite. The leaves are a source of chlorophyll. A good source of carotene (vitamin A) and vitamin K, vitamin C, Niacin, and vitamin B-1. ***Avoid while taking blood-thinning agents.***

ORGANIC KELP, DULSE: Known to contain over 96 different minerals and trace minerals. These foods represent the most potent mineral-rich whole foods. The little known red kelp called Dulse has been reported to restore kidney function, while the iodine in green kelp is helpful for thyroid problems. **Iodine in small amounts is needed in every diet.**

ORGANIC ORANGE PEEL: Orange peel contains higher amounts of certain nutrients than its flesh. For instance, 3.5 ounces of orange peel provides 136 milligrams (mg) of vitamin C, while the flesh contains about 71 mg. Orange peel also contains considerable amounts of Calcium, Copper, Magnesium, vitamin A, Folate and other B vitamins and dietary fiber.

ORGANIC BEET ROOT POWDER: Beet Root Powder provides a wide range of nutrients, but its most significant phytochemical is Betaine. This plant chemical may support liver and kidney health by recycling the amino acid Methionine to maintain the body's stores of S-Adenosyl-Methionine, more commonly known as SAM-e. Betaine may also support the liver's ability to process fat. This may possibly prevent the accumulation of fatty tissues in the liver. Beet roots are sources of Potassium, Phosphorus, Iron, Magnesium and Calcium as well as vitamin A, B and C. Beets have been shown to provide antioxidant, anti-inflammatory, and detoxification.

ORGANIC DANDELION LEAF: An excellent digestive aid and diuretic. Chock full of vitamins A, B, C, and D as well as minerals such as Iron, Potassium, and Zinc.

ORGANIC LEMON PEEL: Lemon peels contain as much as 5 to 10 times more vitamins than the lemon juice itself. To name a few: vitamin C, vitamin A, Beta-carotene, Folate, Calcium, Magnesium, and Potassium.

ORGANIC GINKGO LEAF: Ginkgo leaf is often referred to as a brain herb because of its rich nutrient content and associated health benefits. Ginkgo leaf powder is packed with plant-based antioxidants called Flavonoids, which protect cells and reduce the risk for developing age-related diseases. It is also rich in Terpenoids that researchers believe improve blood flow to the brain.

ORGANIC WHEAT GRASS: Wheat grass is loaded with Beta-carotene, Calcium, Chlorophyll, fiber, Iron and vitamin K. Wheat grass contains an abundance of Chlorophyll, which helps detoxify and cleanse the body while eliminating harmful toxins. Chlorophyll is also the reason wheat grass has an alkalizing effect on the body, balancing pH levels and correcting a build-up of acids, which can inhibit the body's ability to absorb nutrients. This alkalizing process also helps deliver oxygen to your cells, giving you a boost of energy. Wheat grass enhances your body's ability to ward off infections because it contains immune-boosting nutrients like beta-carotene and vitamin C.

Other good greens:

ORGANIC KALE: Kale is also a good source of dietary fiber and an excellent source of vitamin A (in the form of Carotenoids), vitamin K, and Manganese. It is a very good source of copper, Tryptophan, vitamin B-6, and Potassium; and a good source of Magnesium, vitamin E, vitamin B-2, protein, vitamin B-1, Folate, Phosphorous, and vitamin B-3. Also worth noting in Kale's nutritional profile is its vitamin K content. Kale contains nearly twice the amount of vitamin K as most of its fellow cruciferous vegetables.

ORGANIC CHLORELLA: It has the highest concentration of Chlorophyll of any plant known in the world. Chlorella contains protein, carbohydrates, the whole range of B vitamins, vitamin C and E, amino acids and trace minerals. It contains more vitamin B-12 than calf liver does. Chlorella is a great supplement to help boost the immune system and to help the body detoxify as well. It aids in cleansing of the bloodstream.

ORGANIC MORINGA: Moringa is a nutrient rich food that contains 46 antioxidants, 90 nutrients including high quality protein, Calcium, trace minerals, Iron, and all 9 essential amino acids.
Not only does Moringa provide all that nutrition, it also contains powerful antioxidants, and has anti-fungal, antibacterial and anti-inflammatory properties.

Once diet is established, when giving supplements, take at least 1-2 days off a week. I pick Sunday for nothing but meats on that day. I however have two dogs with joint issues so I watch them and if I feel they need joint supplements at that time, I will add those in. Stop supplements at least 1-7 days before having surgery of any type. If joint supplements are important, do not use the day before surgery. Stop vitamin E and fish oils about 7 days prior to having surgery.

Mushrooms (Optional):
Mushrooms are great for detoxing the body. There are at least 270 medicinal mushrooms and there are 7 of the most popular ones you see the most being sold on the market.
Turkey Tail, Chaga, Reishi, Shiitake, Cordyceps, Maitake, and Lion's Mane. Mushrooms work against cancer, arthritis, respiratory, auto immune disease, liver disease, heart disease and lowering cholesterol to name a few. Mushrooms will oxygenate the blood fighting off diseases and building a stronger immune system. You can never go wrong adding mushrooms into the diet. Buy organic. A decent price I found is at *MushroomHarvest.com* with a 14 mushroom blend. It does contain rice flour in which I found many do. There is another that is in

capsules made by Fungiology. The mushrooms are organic as well. Contains organic white milo (sorghum).

Dosage:
0-5 lbs: 1/8-1/4 teaspoon - twice daily
5-10 lbs: 1/4-1/2 teaspoon - twice daily
10-20 lbs: 1/2-1 teaspoon - twice daily
20-50 lbs: 1-2 teaspoons - twice daily
50-75 lbs: 2-3 teaspoons - twice daily
75+ lbs: 4 teaspoons or more - twice daily

Avoid mushrooms when taking prednisone or steroids of any kind. Avoid mushrooms also at least 7 days prior to vaccinating your dog and several days after.

Diatomaceous Earth (Food Grade-only)
Good for many uses. You can even clean house, brush teeth, use for the lawn for killing insects, fleas, ticks etc. Great to add into your dog's food and helps with:

- Detoxing
- Fleas and ticks
- Worming
- Reducing tumors
- Brushing teeth
- Digestive Issues
- Better Organ functions (Heart Murmurs, Kidneys etc)
- Reduction in Seizures
- Allergies
- Hot Spots
- Healthy Shiny Coats

Although this dust is very fine and if using indoors or enclosed places, wear a dust mask and not around your pets. I wouldn't sling it around in the house. Get low to floor to distribute. The particles are very small and sharp and can cut the lungs when inhaling. Otherwise this is extremely safe for ingesting and using externally as well. It has many uses including cleaning.

Dosage:
Under 25 lbs: 1/2 teaspoon
25-50 lbs: 1-2 teaspoons
50-100 lbs: 1 tablespoon
100+ lbs: 1-2 tablespoons
Diatomaceous Earth is less effective in humid environments.

Reference chart when dosage isn't listed:

Herb Dosage

Weight	Tincture	0 Capsule	Tea	Powder
5-10 lbs	2 drops	1/2 cap	1 tsp	1/4 tsp
10-20 lbs	4 drops	1 cap	2 tsp	1/4-1/2 tsp
20-30 lbs	6 drops	1 cap	1 TBSP	1/2 tsp
30-50 lbs	6 drops	2 caps	4 tsp	1/2-1 tsp
50-70 lbs	6-10 drops	2 caps	5 tsp	1 tsp
70-90 lbs	14-18 drops	3 caps	2 TBSP	1 1/2 tsp
90-110 lbs	18-22 drops	4 caps	3 TBSP	2 tsp
110-150 lbs	22-26 drops	4 caps	4 TBSP	2 1/2 tsp
150-180 lbs	26-30 drops	5 caps	5 TBSP	3 tsp

All preparations can be given up to 3 times daily for short term use.

If your dog experiences unusual side effects, substitute with some-thing else. Adverse reactions to the herbs recommended are unusual. But just like people, allergic reactions are possible.

Do not give softgel capsules because dogs have shorter digestive tracts, so these capsules often pass through the GI tract undigested. Avoid tablets as they contain more added junk ingredients (fillers, binders).

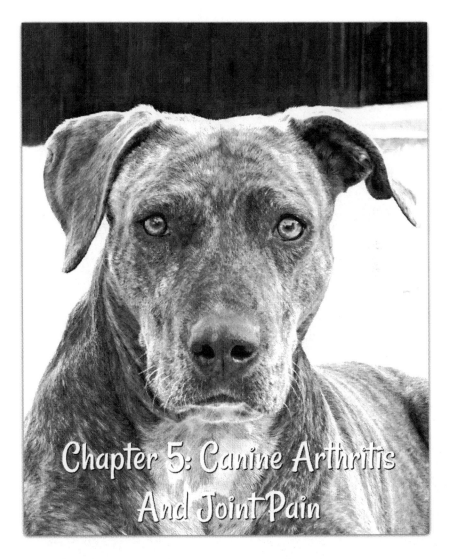

Chapter 5: Canine Arthritis
And Joint Pain

Chapter 5
Canine Arthritis and Joint Pain

When it comes to joint issues, it can be difficult to find the right path to help our babies. All dogs respond to medications, supplements and diet differently. So this isn't set in stone for every dog. This is a basic guide to help you get started in helping your dog to feel better quickly. And not all of these are recommended for one dog. These are just some choices available to you. I believe a good diet, filtered water, correct and balanced supplements, good preservative-free joint supplements, exercise and therapy with minimal to no medications and vaccines is the best way to go.

Before you can prevent the disease you have to understand it.

A Few Precautions:

Drug-induced joint problems:
The drugs most associated with drug-induced lameness are antibiotics, especially **sulfa drugs, Erythromycin, Penicillin's, and Cephalosporin's.** Genetics also play a role in the development of this syndrome as well. Doberman Pinchers are predisposed to develop drug-induced lameness when administered sulfa drugs.

BEWARE OF THE DAMAGING EFFECTS OF INFLAMMATORY DRUGS (NSAIDs):
If your dog is being treated for arthritis, most veterinarians will prescribe steroids and/or non-steroidal anti-inflammatory drugs (NSAIDs). (Steroids and NSAIDs should not be taken together). Physical side effects can be scary - including gastrointestinal bleeding and kidney and liver damage. If your dog's stomach and liver survive prolonged use of NSAIDs, his joints may not. Used long-term, these drugs can destroy the cartilage making the arthritis and pain much worse.

Rimadyl (one of the more popular dispensed NSAIDs) lists as reported possible adverse drug events by the manufacturer: gastrointestinal vomiting, anorexia and/or abnormal stools; pathology of the liver with or without general hepatic dysfunction; neurologic (nerves and brain pathologies), urinary pathologies with increased urination, thirst, increased Blood Urea Nitrogen (BUN), Creatinine and/or abnormal urinalysis; behavioral change; dermatologic (skin problems), immunologic/ allergic pathologies and death. Some reports contained multiple events.
In one study in people in Norway, physicians examined the x-rays of 294 arthritic hips. They found that the hip joints of patients taking NSAIDs had significantly **greater damage** than those not taking the drug.

Steroids like Prednisone, Prednisilone, injectables like Kenalog and Vetalog etc. are devastating to the body over long-term use. They can actually bring on heart disease, diabetes, eye damage, osteoporosis, non-regenerative anemia, weaken the immune defense to disease and upset the body's water and electrolyte balance that weakens the body.

Here is a list of NSAIDs:

RIMADYL (Carprofen) caplets, RIMADYL tablets, and RIMADYL injectable
NOVOCOX (Carprofen) caplets
VETPROFEN (Carprofen) caplets
CARPRIEVE (Carprofen) caplets, CARPRIEVE injection
LIBREVIA (Carprofen) soft chewable tablets; now called QUELLIN (Carprofen) tablets
METACAM (Meloxicam) oral suspension, METACAM injectable
OROCAM (Meloxicam) transmucosal oral spray, Meloxicam injection
LOXICOM (Meloxicam) injection
MELOXIDYL (Meloxicam) oral suspension
Meloxicam Solution - injection
DERAMAXX (Deracoxib) tablets
PREVICOX (Firocoxib) tablets
GALLIPRANT- tablets

All vets recommend NSAIDs for pain. NSAIDs are a very high-risk and a dangerous drug. Many dogs have died from taking these medications. I am not saying that they are not needed in some cases but should only be given short-term, no longer than 2 weeks. (It has been documented that dogs have died after taking the first dose). There is a high possibility not to have to give these for more than a week or at all if you use other means of pain relief depending on the cause of the pain. CanineActiv (mild-moderate) is available without a prescription and completely all-natural. Holistic vets may offer you RJ+. It's the RX version of CanineActiv. It is 100mg stronger.

Also pain meds like Tramadol (moderate pain), Robaxin (muscle relaxer), and Gabapentin (nerve related pain) are somewhat safer than the NSAIDs listed above although these have their side effects as well. The trick is to change everything you have learned and was told. Vets do not have a clue when it comes to natural remedies or even nutrition. Some will recommend therapies like Hydrotherapy. But ALL will send you home with the NSAIDs. And not many vets recommend Adequan which I find baffling to me since it IS an RX medication in which they can prescribe and have access to.

This is why we <u>must</u> find alternatives to what we are told and have been doing. The body works as a whole. You cannot put a band-aid on a pain and expect things to get better. That's all these medications do. If you want your dog to heal and become pain-free or close to it, you <u>must</u> do so much more. There are many steps to heal the body and they must all come together for positive results.

Before prescribing NSAIDs for long-term use, a Heska ERD urine test to look for microalbuminuria, which can be an early sign of kidney disease. If the Heska ERD test is positive, a risk-benefit analysis is used to determine whether to use NSAIDs, or look for other options.

Warning: *Steroids should never be combined with NSAIDs, which should be discontinued for at least 72 hours before switching from either one to the other. They can be combined with all other types of pain medication. When used for more than 4 months, monitoring of blood work and urinalysis should be done.*

Tramadol contains the inactive ingredients Aspartame, Copovidone, Crospovidone, Ethylcellulose, Magnesium Stearate, Mannitol, Mint flavor, and Silicon Dioxide.

**Note that Tramadol should not be given with MAOIs (such as Anipryl/-Deprenyl/Selegiline, and the Preventic tick collar, which contains Amitraz, another MAOI). It should be used with caution when combining with SSRIs (such as Prozac, Zoloft and Paxil) or TCAs (such as Elavil and Clomicalm) due to the risk of serotonin syndrome. It may also be dangerous if combined with St. John's Wort. Tramadol is metabolized 70% thru the liver and 30% thru the kidneys, so dosage must be reduced when using with a dog that has liver or kidney disease. Tramadol in high doses has been known to lead to

seizures. It should be used with extreme caution in animals that are prone to seizures. Tramadol can cause constipation. Give pumpkin if needed.

Vaccine induced

Immune Arthritis is seen in dogs in which the Distemper vaccine may be involved in cases of Immune Arthritis, as Distemper vaccine particles have been found in some of the affected joints. Vaccines play a huge role in illnesses. Consider Titer testing instead.

Diet

I truly believe that diet plays a major role in our dog's health. Remember, in the holistic world of pet care, you focus on repairing and cleansing the whole body. Vets treat with modern treatments and focus on the illness only. It's a band-aid to the real problem within. Vets have no clue about diet or choose not to learn so that they can keep you coming back. You MUST heal the gut. You have to get the digestive system healthy, which in turn builds a strong immune system. If your dog is ill or overcome with arthritis, pain and inflammation, this is where to start. Change the diet; build the immune system by repairing the gut and organs.

So let's say your dog has arthritis or some joint disease and now we have to spend that extra time and money in our busy lives to help our dogs be pain-free or comfortable. A lot of work. Do you see where I am going with this? Think about all the visits to the vet to help your dog when he/she is hurting. If we had known in the early years that diet played a role in joint issues, we may have made extra time to pay attention to the diet. If you are lucky enough to have a younger dog without issues yet, maybe it's time to concentrate on the diet now. Start now thinking about what you can do for your dog **before** it takes on the pains of arthritis. And if they are already ridden by the joint pain and inflammation, let's make some changes today starting right now.

IF you are feeding kibble, I hope by reading the earlier chapters of this book that you have already decided to change your dog's diet. Start now by getting your dog (if they are not already) on a good preservative-free joint supplement. Add in some vitamins and minerals.

Watch the diet for potatoes, sugars, preservatives, corn, soy, wheat and all grains including feeding of kibble or commercial pet foods. Carbohydrates (corn, wheat, rice, soy, millet and even potato) are pro-inflammatory foods; they promote inflammation. All herbs are an optional alternative and it may take awhile to see the best results in some cases. Start with a joint support supplement according to the severity. I find a good combination of ingredients works the very best.

The Power of Massage
What you can do for your dog at home is give him/her a massage. A daily massage will keep blood circulating in the areas where arthritis is a problem, as well as contribute to better blood flow throughout the entire body. Your dog will truly love the attention and enjoy the time you spend with him/her. Take 5-10 minutes (depending on your dog) of your day, sit down on the floor or bed and rub your baby. When you keep the muscles relaxed, there is less pressure on the joints trying to pull the bones out of place, especially the spine. Even rub the paws and, if your dog will let you, work in-between the toes. If you get in the habit of massages, they may eventually let you rub in-between, which also helps when it comes time for a nail trimming.

Vet Checks with Injuries and Arthritis
When you suspect a joint issue or lameness in your dog, you take your dog in to see the vet. I find a lot of times people come to me after they have taken their dog in and the vet didn't do x-rays but yet diagnosed the dog with arthritis or hip dysplasia or whatever joint may be hurting at the time without doing much needed x-rays. Wait what? If you suspect a problem with a joint, it **should** be x-rayed immediately so that you know what you are dealing with. You cannot treat something if you don't have the correct diagnosis. A guessing vet isn't going to cut it. This happens so many times that it frustrates the vets that actually DO care about their patients and do get x-rays right away so they know how to treat the dog. This is beyond my compre-hension that vets wouldn't do x-rays. Laziness perhaps or in a hurry and doesn't have time for you. Either way it is unacceptable!

Ok for an example; your dog is limping and you are concerned so you take your dog to the vet and the vet says, "Oh your dog has a sprained wrist" or "Your dog has arthritis in his back" and sends you home with pain medication without doing any tests or x-rays. REALLY? Is this your kind of vet? If so, fire him/her and find a new one right away. This vet not only put you off, but also didn't have a care in the world on how to help your dog. If you find your vet hesitating, request x-rays. Don't wait for your vet to suggest it. You need a proper diagnosis to be able to treat the dog correctly. I am finding this happening a lot more than it should and it really has me concerned for pet parents and of course the welfare of the dog. This is why I want you to know so that when/if you walk into a clinic one day with a lame dog, you will know what to do and what to expect. If for any reason your vet is not willing to work with you on ALL levels, by all means find a new one. They are a dime a dozen.

Just because you like them because they are polite to you or nice to your dog doesn't make them an ideal vet. You are the one paying the bill. It is YOUR dog. You have every say-so on what happens when you walk through those doors. Same goes for your children and so does it for your pets. You want the best care for your dog so find the best vet for you and your pets.

Having What You Need
Make sure you have all the right supplements including a joint sup-plement. In these supplements, make sure there aren't any preserva-tives or artificial fillers or additives and there are many out there that are full of this junk. Go for the smallest amount possible with pre-servatives. Sometimes they can't be avoided but knowing which ones are the worst, is also crucial. Find a good mix of substances. Giving just Glucosamine/Chondroitin isn't your best bet. I find supplements that have a combination of good ingredients work the best or you can give several joint supplements with different ingredients. Add in high quality fish oil (sardine, green lipped mussel or squid), Ester C (Mag-nesium Ascorbate) along with a mix of anti inflammatory herbs. Better yet, go with the all-natural form and add in Rosehips or Camu Camu. These contain the highest concentration of natural vitamin C than any other food. Vitamin C (Ascorbic Acid) is synthetic so it's harder for the body to absorb and you are risking the product being from China, as most all (95%) vitamin C in the USA is sourced from China. Boswellia, Turmeric, Ginger, Yucca and Devil's Claw are just a couple of some really good herbs that work well. Add Milk Thistle to help filter the liver from all the toxins in his/her body. If your dog

is limping from arthritis, a moist heat pack 3 times a day for 20 minutes helps relieve some of the pain. If there is a new injury or inflammation or you just took a walk and your dog is limping more, use an ice pack for 20 minutes 3 times a day for the first 72 hours. You can also alternate moist cold and heat packs. In winter it's great for helping with stiff joints using moist heat therapy. Keep your dog warm so the joints won't ache too much.

For extreme pain, give the pain meds you received from the vet or better yet, try a supplement called CanineActiv (found on *CanineArthritisAndJoint.com* website) to go along with your joint supplements. Increase the amount of the recommended dosage on your joint supplements as well.

If that isn't enough, there is a good combo I like. When a dog is hurting, I go straight for the anti-inflammatory herbs mix, Glucosamine with mixed ingredients, CanineActiv, TRF 150 and CBD oil. Also a liquid form of homeopathic herbs mix with Arnica, Ruta and Calendula. I do everything I can to keep from giving any pain meds if the pain isn't so severe that they are showing clear signs like whining and/or struggling to even take a step.

Try not to give NSAIDs any longer than 2 weeks if you must give them. Actually NSAIDs break down cartilage and make the joints even worse so try to stay away from these as much as possible but please, if your dog is in horrible pain, by all means, give them something for pain if needed and know the risks involved. Even one dose can be deadly so use extreme caution and make sure you are ready for any deathly consequences. Ask your vet how he would treat a severe reaction to NSAIDs and what you can watch for in an emergency. As far as I know, there isn't one. I also have found vets to deny these claims even though they know the risks involved with these medications.

Adequan works well also when you have a dog that has chronic joint issues. It takes up to 4 weeks (sometimes longer) to kick in but it is well worth it once you get the body primed with it. Giving injections at home is much cheaper. Adequan is not to be given to dogs with kidney disease or diabetes. Check with your vet about getting you a prescription for possibly ordering online, as it is cheaper that way most of the time. If my vet gave them, it would cost me $35-$40 per injection. If I give them at home, it's about $15 per injection. Well worth learning how to give one. Have your vet show you how.

There are many questions on whether to give subcutaneous injection (Sub Q) or in the muscle (IM). Per manufactures recommendations it should be injected into the muscle. The reason for this is, it takes effect a lot faster being injected into the muscle. So make a note of that if your vet recommends Sub Q. I give in muscle and that's how I will always do it.

Don't let your dog jump off of beds, couches, out of vehicles or jump-ing at any extent if your dog is in pain or has severe joint issues. I never let my special needs girl jump out of my vehicle or in playing. I lift all 70 lbs of her and sit her down on the ground. When she gets in the truck, I put her front feet on the seat and support her rear evenly and lift her slowly to get her even with the seat then let her move for-ward to get in the back seat. I don't have a backdoor for my truck's backseat, as it is an older model, so she has to go over the console. You may find a ramp or something to do this a lot easier but this is what I do. She doesn't move without me helping her either. She knows the routine.

Rest works well for an arthritic dog in pain. Once the pain has subsided, take daily short walks (5-6 houses down and back if possible). You can work up to further walks but do not push it. You can do several short walks daily. Again you can use CanineActiv for that extra support during times that your dog may be pushed to walk for exercise or has over-extended themselves. Don't forget your ice packs.

If you have a doggie door, make sure it fits your dog properly. A dog constantly ducking its head or having to squeeze through a small door will make the problems much worse. Or having to step 6 inches up and over. The pet door should be low at the bottom of the door. Keep slick floors covered with non-slip rugs so your dog doesn't slip or have to work hard to stay on all fours. They also make non-slip doggie boots. I use these for going to the vet or for therapy as they always have the slick floors.

Water therapy works very well (2-3 times a week is ideal). It's one of the best things you can do for an arthritic or injured dog. Don't forget your chiropractor and acupuncturist. There are so many things you can do to help your dog and it doesn't have to cost a fortune. Find what works for you and your dog and work at helping him/her be a happy pup again. You can also do an Epsom Salt bath. If your dog is really having a tough time and you can get him in the tub without causing further pain or injury, let them sit in a tub of warm water with Epsom salts. Help those achy joints. Or a small kiddie pool outside (during warmer weather of course) with warm water and add in Epsom salts. Even aluminum free baking soda (most are including Arm & Hammer) in the bath along with Epsom salts is refreshing, helps relieve itching and absorbs toxins from the body.

As for Hydrotherapy, you will find vets and surgeons that will tell you to wait 8 weeks at least of rest before walking, doing Hydrotherapy or anything. In speaking with my therapist, he says this is where therapists and vets/surgeons don't agree. He feels the sooner you can get them into therapy, the quicker the recovery. I agree on this and this is why. If you end up having knee surgery, the next day, they have you up walking around the hospital. Then they want you in therapy as soon as possible. So why is it vets and surgeons are taught differently? Makes you wonder. I don't have a good reason but in my personal opinion and what I have gone through with my dog, I think getting the dog walking as soon as possible is better for a quicker recovery. I will give you examples.

When Sydney, my big girl had an unknown issue with her right knee/leg bowing out, we laid around for a month before I started her on therapy. By then, she had no muscle left in that leg. She almost couldn't walk due to muscle wasting. So when she tore her ACL/CCL here a few months ago, the vet told me 8 weeks rest. I knew when he said it that was **not** going to happen. I let her rest for 4 weeks and we headed off to Hydrotherapy. BUT during this rest time I massaged her daily. I loaded her up on all of her supplements. Nothing seemed to help but I knew in my mind it was helping in some way. I started her back on Adequan that I had stopped giving her 2 months earlier. Bad

90

mistake on my part! The ACL/CCL is slowly healing but she is using her muscles during Hydrotherapy so she has strength to walk on her own and recover quicker. It brought us to the point of being able to take walks without causing much pain and less chance of re-injury. In other words, Hydrotherapy gave us time for the knee to start healing and repairing itself. It creates scar tissue around it and forms some sort of support again. We did not choose surgery for several reasons. My therapist isn't in favor of surgery. He has even seen surgery patients not recover well at all and sometimes come out worse. Get to know your surgeon. I will say every single dog and case is different. It depends on the size of your dog, the activity of your dog, the extent of the ACL/CCL tear and age and health issues of your dog. Second, I didn't have $3,000. So alternative therapy was our only option.

I purchased a soft leg brace for her and it has really helped a lot. At first I didn't see much of a difference but now I am seeing a big difference. She can really be struggling to walk and I put her brace on and she can walk a lot better and faster. (I keep having this thought in my head from the movie Forrest Gump, "Lt. Dan got new legs. Ha!") She just tired out quick in the beginning which is understandable and is common with any injury and after lying around for a month. We have also started short walks with braces on. I purchased one for both legs so to try to help deter a second ACL tear and it is also her knee that bows out. So we walked ten houses down and back at first. We have gone up to 1/2 mile but I may need to drop back on that a little since this last walk caused her some pain. How do I know she was in pain when she never makes a sound and never shows pain?? Because she is limping much harder (head bobbing). It's understandable to limp harder after the walk but the next day, the walking should be back to normal; whatever normal is at that time. We do some P.R.O.M. exercises and daily massages along with chiropractic adjustments, Class 3b laser therapy and sound wave therapy at home. It's been a lot of work. All of this you will have to do if you choose surgery or if you don't. We just skipped the surgery part. Sometimes ACL tears don't heal well even after 6 months even without surgery so then you may consider surgery if it's in your budget. I know some dogs that haven't had surgery and it took a year to actually get back to normal. Time and patience is critical on your part. It's not an easy recovery.

I had a few things that happened a couple years ago that I was unsure if I was onto something or just thinking crazy things. The first time that was the worst is when Diamond (my oldest girl) went down (in severe pain and couldn't walk). I had adopted her a year earlier. I took her into the vet and nothing was discovered from the vet. It was brushed off as a stomach ache. Needless to say not much was done either on that visit. We came back home and she was fine a day or two then back down again. A week later I took her back in for x-rays thinking possibly she may have hip dysplasia. The x-rays confirmed she had Lumbosacral Spondylosis. At the time, I had no clue what that was and didn't take it that serious. A few days before I took her in on the first visit, I had started giving her some Cephalexin for a UTI. When I discovered how bad she was in pain, I stopped everything. After she was back up and walking a day or two later, I started the antibiotics up again. That's when she went back down again and I took her for x-rays. This was in March. In November of that same year I took her in for a teeth cleaning (different vet), a Rabies shot, and blood work. Little did I know at that time, you don't give Rabies on the same day you do surgery (things vets won't tell you). Three days after her teeth cleaning she went down again and she went down hard. This was November 2012. Since that day it had been nothing but a daily struggle to keep her pain-free. I took her back to the vet when she went down and I told them it had something to do with the surgery. I told them I thought she had had a reaction to antibiotics previously. They looked at me like I had two heads. Since then I have spoken with many vets about this. The only thing that was mentioned is the possibility of the bacteria could have caused it that was released from the teeth cleaning, or possibly the anesthesia but we just really didn't know.

In the back of my mind I have wondered if the connection was the antibiotics. The vets looked at me crazy when I kept mentioning my thoughts on this. So when I met my new vet to discuss her Stem Cell surgery, I told him all of this and how it has put her down (in severe pain daily) since the teeth cleaning. So he was concerned about the anesthesia and would make sure he didn't give any antibiotics etc. So, she had the surgery and it didn't put her down at all. So now I know it wasn't the anesthesia.

I was reading a book on Canine Arthritis (that was written by a DVM) and BINGO...there it was, my answer.

ANTIBIOTICS!

It states: *While RARE, many doctors feel that drug-induced joint problems are becoming more common. Your dog's immune system can react to ANY drug, and drugs are usually considered foreign substances. A hypersensitivity or allergic reaction occurs when antibodies form chemical complexes with the administered drug, these drug-antibody complexes are then deposited into the joints of the body. The drugs most commonly associated with drug-induced lameness are antibiotics, especially sulfa drugs, Erythromycin, Penicillin, and Cephalosporin's.*

It further states genetics can play a role also especially with Doberman Pinchers when sulfa drugs are administered.

SO, when I read this, my jaw dropped and my thoughts were, I was right, I WASN'T CRAZY! So why didn't these vets **not** put this together or even possibly think it was drug-related? They have this knowledge right? Maybe they knew and chose not to tell me.
I can give Diamond Doxycycline and Clindamycin without any issues but Cephalexin puts her down. Looking back in her records on the day she had her teeth cleaning, she was given an injection of Penicillin and sent home with Amoxicaps. So obviously she has sensitivity to these as well. The bad part about this is, it put her down from November until the day of her stem cell therapy (Sept 12th the next year). Ten months of pain.
Why so many antibiotics? It's just a teeth cleaning. Skip the antibiotics and when you get come home, do oral mouth rinses using Probiotics and Colloidal Silver.

Note.- Pets allergic to antibiotic class of Penicillin will naturally be allergic to Amoxicillin as well. Please make sure your pet's veterinarian is aware of this.

And not only am I speaking about medications, but vaccines can also do this. Even vaccines can make a dog go lame that's never had any issues before, although it seems more common in puppies. Like the distemper vaccine; particles have been found in joints. I am not ruling out adults as well. Vaccines are very harmful in adult stages and titer testing should be done instead. Titer (Vaccicheck or Kansas State University is the cheapest way-ask your vet) costs a little more money but if you have a dog that gets ill, goes lame or acquires a disease, which one then will be expensive? So weigh the costs. Have titer testing done instead. I am aware Rabies is a law but every 3 years this should be the most that gets done. Find a vet that offers a 3-year option vaccine. Some want you back in every year so they can make money. Where did this mindset come from? And if your dog has an illness, weakened immune system or autoimmune disease, they can and should be exempted from Rabies. Speak with your vet about this to see what can be done.

The bottom line here is, always be aware of what goes in the body and don't think your suspicions are crazy or a little over the top. Always trust your instincts, ask a lot of questions, research before you have any surgery done or vaccines and medications given. And always feed your dog a species-appropriate diet. Don't forget filtering the water. Anytime the body is fighting any disease or illness, inflammation can flow through the body causing inflamed joints.

Also note: During wintertime this is a time for our dogs to start having achy joints. So get ready before. Prepare. Have your medicine cabinet stocked with meds (preferably all natural like CanineActiv and TRF 150), herbs (start the herbs before winter if you haven't), vitamins and minerals and don't forget the ADEQUAN. It's wonderful stuff and can make miracles when you have lost all hope. It did for me and has helped many animals stay upright and walking. Ask your vet for a vial to take home with you to give the injections. Have on hand some moist heat/cold packs, funds saved up for chiropractic, water therapy and acupuncture visits. Give daily massages and take short walks. Watch your dog's weight and if you're not already, consider feeding a raw diet. You will be totally amazed how much your dog will be so much healthier. A raw diet won't fix your dog with joint issues but it will certainly help.

If your dog has had any type of trauma or injury, participates in any type of agility or repetitive exercises; your dog should be on a joint supplement. When playing with your dog, don't tug on any part of the body too hard. For example, playing tug of war with your dog will put some stress on the neck and possibly pull the spinal bones out of line causing injury. Don't forget to make sure you have studied the breed of dog you have and know the genetic history concerning hip dysplasia, degenerative joint disease and alike. If your breed is susceptible to diseases of the joints, take action now while they are young (6 months). There is so much to do to keep your dog moving way into his/her teen years. Remove kibble from the diet. Reduce all vaccines, medications, change to organic all-natural yard fertilizers, and use all-natural flea and tick repellants and shampoos. Do not apply topical flea and tick killers. They ARE killers to your dog.

Now what I would like to discuss is, what makes our dogs with joint issues go from bouncy and pain-free to all of a sudden in pain and can't move. Well if you haven't pinpointed what causes a flare up, take a look at everything you have done for your dog. If you haven't missed anything mentioned above then consider other things, for example the weather. The weather wreaks havoc on us humans and it affects our pets the same.

A lot of the time the barometric pressure can drop causing the body to react and the joints will start to ache. Damp days of humidity followed by cold fronts are a big aggravator. It can start a few days earlier, so if you know it's coming, give a little extra joint supplement, therapy, and/or massage a day or two before this arrives.

If your dog has some type of infection going on, say the ear or tooth, expect the joints to become inflamed as well and cause pain and swelling in the arthritic joints. Any time you have an infection, it causes bacteria to travel throughout the body and affect the weakest parts of the body. If your dog has itchy skin with lesions or is inflamed and red, expect the joints to be hurting as well. Everything that happens to one part of the body, affects the rest of the body. Bacteria attacks weak points in the body's immune system. The best things you can do for your dog is keep his/her system strong. So have a list of what is specific to your dog as how to care for your dog daily and then prepare for the worst days when something goes wrong. If your dog has a heart problem, giving herbs for the heart can also work for the arthritis. Herbs are good for many different uses and you will find that when you're helping the heart, you're helping the joints.

As I said, the body works in sync and you have to treat every issue so not to affect the other. Again these supplements can and do benefit an older dog and one with joint issues. Every dog is different and everything out there that helps one dog may not help another, so it is a constant job of trying to find that right mixture that helps. And as luck would have it, once you find that right mixture, it stops working and so here you are looking for a different solution. This is why it is important to learn everything you can so that you have options when that day comes.

What To Do When Your Dog Has Had Surgery Or Is Lame

1. First of all, put rubber-backed rugs down everywhere if you have tile/hardwood/vinyl floors. Your dog will have an extremely hard time walking on these types of floors. Don't take a chance on them re-injuring themselves. I have found the thin rubber-backed carpet that you can cut to fit for around $60 for 5x6 sizes. I cut it to the size I need. You can find this at TownhouseLinens.com called Royale wall to wall bathroom carpet and rugs by Mohawk. Cut to size you want and wash in non-chemical laundry detergent. Dry on delicate cycle using Meyer's dryer sheets or organic wool dryer balls.

2. Keep any other pets from pushing or shoving your dog around. They can re-injure your lame dog. Teach your other dogs they cannot push. This is teaching respect for others.

3. When your dog needs to go to the potty, walk with him. If s/he is an active dog that likes to run, put a short leash on so s/he can't. No running while the body is healing.

4. Every day you will need to do leg exercises and massage. Per your vet or your therapists home instructions of course but massage will not hurt your dog. Be gentle and rub the muscle and skin. As you are able to do leg exercises, do these in short intervals 2-3 times daily or recommended by your orthopedic vet or therapist.

5. Try to slowly taper off risky NSAIDs or other pain meds. After 2 weeks, hopefully your dog will no longer need any pain medications. Add in some herbs specific for joint and inflammation issues. Don't forget to give CanineActiv a try as well. Yes you may give these while giving NSAIDs as well but the goal is to wean off of the prescription pain meds as soon as possible. Increase the joint supplement dosage. Add in anti-inflammatory herbs. Fish oils help along with glucosamine's.

6. Do water therapy when sutures have been removed or healed. Water therapy (Hydrotherapy) is good at all times and for all issues. It has the power to help heal your dog along with re-building muscle and strength and helps your dog to lose weight for those that are a little pudgy.

7. Make sure you have your dog on a very good joint supplement that does not contain preservatives or a very small amount. If you are unsure, I keep an updated list on my Canine Arthritis and Joint website so you will know what to look for. I even have a list of ingredients to avoid.

8. Start your dog on Adequan injections immediately. Make sure they do not have kidney disease or diabetes. Speak with your vet. You can get it online cheaper than what the vets sell a vial for usually, but giving it at home is your cheapest route. Have your vet show you how to give a shot and buy the **equine** version. It's at least $15 cheaper a vial. The loading dose will be the most costly so buying Equine version is most cost-effective. The only difference is, the Canine version has a preservative in it for longer shelf life and the Equine version does not. I have two dogs on it and I buy the equine version and still do to this day. And of course, the bigger the dog, the more you will use from the vial. I can get 2-3 injections per vial. That's for 70 lb dogs. The loading dose says twice a week for four weeks then you will gradually work into once a month. That is just not possible in my household. First, Diamond with severe Spondylosis took two months with twice a week injections before I started to see an improvement. To this day, both dogs get an injection every 2 1/2-3 weeks. To find out where your dog's point is, is to wait and watch closely. As you extend the time out, if you see limping, slowing down or just not right with them,

give an injection. If the next day your dog is back to being peppy and feeling good, then that's where your limit is. Find that happy place and stay with it. In winter you may need to watch this as well so you don't need to go completely by the book on the timing. Make your dog comfortable but be smart. It beats the alternative. In the beginning an injection lasts 3 days only until it gets built up into the system. That's why you can start to back off on the injections given per week or month as it builds up in the system.

Sydney has Hip Dysplasia and Spondylosis and even though she gets an injection every 2 1/2-3 weeks as well, she still has a slight bunny hop.
So I give her the CanineActiv and it gets completely rid of her bunny hop. She can walk longer distances too. I give at least 2 caps a day but she does well with 4 caps on her bad days. Some dogs will need to stay on 4 caps a day for maintenance dose. I have seen in extremely painful days, you can increase the amount to 6 caps per day. It won't harm your dog. If your dog doesn't take capsules, you can open these up and sprinkle into food. Do not mix in water. I use these mostly for those "off " days and not as a daily supplement due to costs. They may be a bit bitter but mask it with a dash of garlic or sardines or something your dog likes to mask the smell and taste. The caps, when opened, you can twist and turn them and tap on plate or bowl. It does kind of get stuck in the capsules at times so you must work it out. I have been putting the caps into the raw foods and they haven't found them.

9. For traveling, make sure you do not allow your dog to jump into or out of your vehicle. Lift your dog into and help out of the vehicle. Or invest in a ramp if they can go up ramps easily. Allow plenty of room for them to lie down and be comfortable in your vehicle.
If they are in a crate at times when you are away, make sure the crate has adequate space for moving around in and not just laying in one small space and put orthopedic memory foam in the bottom (you can buy anywhere for humans also and cut it to fit) so the dog will be very comfortable in there. I buy 2-inch thick toppers. Put a thin blanket/throw over the foam. Take them out of the overly-sized crate and walk them every couple of hours. DO NOT crate your dog all day. The amount of time for crating any dog is 4-5 hours. The dog needs to

come out of the crate and walk around and have some interaction. This includes healthy dogs.

Have good orthopedic dog beds all over the house for your dog's favorite spots. If the dog is large and usually sleeps in the bed with you, you will need to lift the dog yourself up onto the bed (supporting the hips or backend if that's where your joint issues are. Keep everything in line so it doesn't shift the body and hurt them more) or the best place is on an orthopedic pet bed next to your bed so he/she doesn't decide they want to jump off of your bed. It is safer on the floor. You can try a ramp or stairs for getting on the bed but these don't always work well either and are just as difficult to get up and down.

10. If you have stairs in your home, you will have to work something out so that your dog does not under any circumstances use the staircase. They do make full body support harnesses. Invest in one if you can. Sleep downstairs with the dog if you have to. Put up a child safety gate. Anything to keep them off those stairs.

11. No Jumping, No Running, No sudden or jerky moves!

This is a basic guide to help you through the healing process. Remember; never let a vet tell you water therapy won't work. It works in ALL cases. Trust me on this one! And the sooner you can start the better. Speak with the therapist that will be doing the therapy and get a time frame set with him/her.
Once arthritis has become fully developed to the point where we have active joint degeneration and/or excess bone formation, we can't cure them but we can certainly make them comfortable throughout their lifetime and live a close to normal life. What I hope for is to reduce your dog's pain so that he/she can move around relatively pain-free, and create a healing environment around the joints so the animal's natural healing abilities can work their own miracles.
Sometimes holistic therapies take a while before results can be seen, so don't give up too soon. And also, understand that you will have to continue with the herbs and other treatments throughout the dog's lifetime.

I am confident we can improve your dog's quality of life for the time they have remaining, and I am happy to know that with the holistic approach, I am helping you and your dog without causing harm.

Walking Your Dog and Exercise
All dogs need some form of exercise. It's good for their overall physical and mental health. When joints hurt, it's harder for them to do a lot of exercise. According to the severity of each dog, take short walks as often as possible without causing the dog any pain or overdoing it. Like Diamond, she started out walking about 6 houses down and back, some days a little further. On the way back though, she walked at a snail's pace. So pay close attention and don't overdo it or you could cause more pain and problems. Keep any excess weight off also. Weight can cause more problems as well. Diamond is now on Adequan and good joint supplements and a raw diet and she is able to walk a mile now. She is doing exceptionally well considering the severity of her disease.

This is one thing that is important for your dog, whether he/she has joint issues or is healthy, young and vibrant. Let me be honest and say, I hate exercise and walking included. I really haven't ever been an exercise person so I must say, my dogs have me walking and I know it is good for me and so my dogs are good for me in more ways than I could mention. And it is good for your dogs too. Dogs require exercise for so many reasons. Spirit, longevity and stress relief.

Like children, they can get cabin fever and need to burn off some energy. If your dog is digging, chewing, or destroying things, your dog needs exercise! Even a dog with fears and aggression need to get exercise. It helps on so many levels. Now with dogs that have joint issues, we must make some adjustments. Dogs with joint issues cannot walk or play like a normal dog. These are the dogs I am going to refer to in this discussion. If your dog has joint issues and is use to walking five miles a day when healthy, that same dog may not be able to walk near that far now. Every single dog is different but you must be aware and know the signs when you have pushed your dog too far. If your dog is in pain or limping before you ever start, that dog should only walk a short distance or not walk at all that day. A short distance is approximately 50 yards and back. If your dog is not limping and having no pain but has severe hip dysplasia, your dog may walk 100 yards and back up to about 1/2 a mile. If your dog is used to walking a mile without any pain during or after that walk, your dog can handle that walk. You have to pay very close attention to your dog's body language as to how your dog is feeling.

If your dog has really bad hips (hip dysplasia) and you walk your dog two miles, you may be putting more wear and tear on that joint than what needs to be happening. So, do not over-walk your dog no matter how your dog is feeling.

Now with Spondylosis, you may be able to walk further without issues because the hips are doing the work because the Spondylosis is in the spine. The spine is moving back and forth and sometimes those bone spurs can poke the spinal nerves and cause more pain so you have to pay attention to your dog. Same goes for ACL tears, luxating patella's etc. So every case is different and unique in its own self. Just please do not try to walk your dog five or ten miles EVER! Not a dog with joint issues. Those days are over for walking that distance. No marathons ok?

For people, we need to walk three miles a day for health purposes. You can try and walk your dog two or three times a day with several shorter walks totaling up to two miles but I do not recommend pushing your dog if the dog is doing well with one mile or even 100 yards.

Why push the dog and take a chance on causing pain and inflammation? It's not worth it! Make sure he/she is getting their joint supplements and you can even give the CanineActiv an hour or two before your walk and give more later that evening. So I hope you are getting my point. When someone says to me that their dog is getting short walks, a short walk could be three miles. That's not short ok?

Here let me break down walks so we are on the same page:
Short walk: up to 50 yards (5 minutes)
Medium walk: up to 100 yards (10 minutes)
Long walk: up to 1 mile (20 minutes)
Extra long walks: over 1 mile (30+ minutes)

So stick with this list and know what is too far and what isn't. Don't over walk your dog. I brought this up when I recently spoke with someone that has a dog in severe pain and walks her dog about **10** miles a day. Oh My God, NEVER EVER do that to a lame dog. It takes a special dog to walk that far even in the healthiest dogs without joint issues. That's like walking a marathon. Don't do this please! By the way, after speaking with her she has reduced her dog's walks to at least half. I am hoping she will reduce it more for the dog's sake.

If you are interested in Homeopathy..here are some products.
Homeopathy - Arnica 200 (Try not to touch the pellets. If you do, make sure your hands are clean)
Arnica and Symphytum are available in the 200c, all others will be in the 30c strength. When using the 30c, administer one dose, then wait an hour and dose again. This seems to deep-seat the remedy. Arnica and Hypericum helps with pain can lessen bleeding and bruising under the skin and is great for sprains and muscle injuries.

Other remedies for Arthritis, joint issues, tendons and ligaments - Homeopathic herbs:

- Rhus Tox
- Hypericum
- Bryonia
- Symphytum
- Ruta Graveolens
- Ledum

I must confess, I have a small issue with the pellets. None I have seen are organic. Organic being for the inactive ingredients such as sucrose (sugar) and corn starch (GMO).) (Hylands brand has lactose and Acacia Gum.) If you use these short term, I am ok with it since the amount of sucrose/corn starch is relatively low. I know people swear by homeopathic and are 100% safe but many vets, holistic vets, holistic Drs and alike do not consider inactive ingredients nor are they looking for organic. I would **love** to see organic pellets/tabs in our near future. This is why I am suggesting a different form of homeopathic in which I have not researched further but may also contain other unwanted ingredients such as alcohol, Potassium Sorbate or

Citric Acid to name a few. Avoid these types of liquid forms. I am only bringing this to your attention so that you are aware. It isn't easy to find things that don't have JUNK ingredients but try to find the best ones. I like buying organic herbal powders because of this. Because most are all pure and organic from herbal companies and will always be my preferred choice although homeopathic has no interactions and are 100% safe in all situations. You can add these into foods or you can either put pellets in the mouth or put into a glass bottle, add filtered water, shake, let dissolve then squirt into your dog's mouth using a syringe, spray or dropper. Keep refrigerated up to 2 weeks.

Types of Glucosamine to Avoid:
Glucosamine alone is ok, but you should avoid Glucosamine Sulfate * NaCL (or KCl) (or if the ingredients list says Potassium or Salt after the Sulfate). Some companies are very tricky about this - **unless it just says Glucosamine Sulfate or HCL**, you likely are getting an inferior product. It is easy for people to see the Glucosamine Sulfate and simply ignore the KCl on the end. We are not all molecular scientists after all. The NaCl and KCl ("the salts") refer to even more (unneeded but cheaper) carrier molecules that can be up to 30% of the product's weight. Some carrier molecule is needed (such as sulfate or HCL alone) because raw Glucosamine is unstable by itself - it needs to be bound to the Sulfate or HCL carrier in order to be stored for any period of time. So if you have one of the KCl or NaCl forms of the Sulfate when you think you are buying a quality product, you are actually getting 30% of your dose as ordinary table salt. Be advised to watch out for products with those markings. The less active amounts of glucosamine you get, the slower your relief will be. At some point it will likely be so low that you will get no benefit at all. NAG (N-Acetylglucosamine or N-Acetyl-D-Glucosamine), is another rare form of Glucosamine but should generally be avoided due to its relative ineffectiveness and expense.

What Kind of Glucosamine Should I Buy?
There are so many different forms and types and brands of Glucosamine out there and the quality varies widely. It is advised that one seek out a reputable manufacturer (one that offers a full, no questions asked, money back guarantee) and follows the old rule of, you get what you pay for. It can also be helpful to look at the label before you

buy or get recommendations from other people you know that use Glucosamine and don't contain junk ingredients. Glucosamine in tablet form is not recommended due to low absorption issues.

Functions:
Although Glucosamine HCl is normally found in shellfish, it can also be created from the fermentation of corn. Glucosamine is necessary in the body for the structure and function of the articular cartilage. It assists in maintaining the elasticity and integrity of the connective tissue and assists in building, maintaining and repairing cartilage, tendons and ligaments. It is most commonly used as a topical ointment or oral supplement to treat Osteoarthritis. The same anti-inflammatory and elasticity properties that make it a great treatment for Osteoarthritis may also contribute to its use in skin products and cosmetics. It's also been known to help in the treatment of Psoriasis.

If your dog has a new injury like an ACL tear, rest is best for at least 4 weeks. Use PROM (passive range of motion) exercises and do daily massages. Pay special attention to rubbing up and down the spine and on the sides of it as well as it is the lifeline to the limbs.
I do recommend giving it a couple of weeks of rest until you know your dog isn't in a lot of pain or is doing better mentally and physically as possible. Then start PROM. Go slow!

What is P.R.O.M.? I will answer that later in this chapter.

After four weeks, get your dog in a pool for swim therapy or find a facility that offers water therapy. It can be a pool or underwater treadmill. Laser therapy, acupuncture, chiropractic all work well too. Use several different means of therapy to get a faster recovery for your dog. Once walking without pain and has little to no limping, do short walks. If they do well and not limping hard that day or the next day, you can do that walk for a week then slightly increase the walks to a little further. Do NOT overdo these walks. Find a distance that works well for your dog. **There should not be hard limping or pain before the walks.** Give CanineActiv before and after the walks will help.
Invest in a pool; say an above ground pool just deep enough for your dog to paddle his legs. Even a pool when the water comes up to the

top of the legs can work very well. Buy a life vest as well if the water is deeper than what they can walk on. It helps a lot, it really does. If they get tired and stop swimming, they won't sink wearing a life vest. Never leave your dog alone in a pool that is deeper than they are. Start the swimming out slow. Say 5-8 minutes of swimming the first time. You can increase that as you go as they progress. Always try to extend your therapy slowly and back off if you see a setback. Don't push it. You will get there. It just may take some time. Continue therapy year round for chronic issues but you can reduce the amount as your dog starts to get better. Walk your dog at least 3 times a week. Swim as much as you like. During wintertime, use a therapy facility for indoor swimming, laser etc. Keep your dog moving. That's the key. If you can find one in your area, hyperbaric oxygen chambers work well for faster healing too. It provides more oxygen in the body therefore supplying the limbs with more circulation and faster healing. It also works well on cancer. It has wonderful healing properties beyond your imagination.

If your dog has Osteoarthritis or a tendon injury that doesn't seem to recover, look into Stem Cell therapy or PRP (Platelet Rich Plasma). Stem cell does cost but your dog shouldn't need any meds afterwards and can function as a normal dog and wouldn't need another injection for a year or two. You must bank the fat cells though and you pay for them to be stored as well. PRP is much cheaper and a great tool for older dogs that cannot go under anesthesia.

For stem cell, your dog will require surgery like being spayed to remove the fat cells. It is somewhat costly but it is completely natural and nothing foreign is going into the body. I tried it on Diamond even though results were unknown for her Spondylosis. It was a 50-50 chance. It worked for four months. A year later though we did another injection and it lasted six months. This was good results for her having Spondylosis and no research done on it. But it does work well on Osteoarthritis. Hip Dysplasia is a 50-50 shot as well. They haven't progressed far enough into helping all dogs at this time but they are striving to help in the future. There is also PRP (Platelet Rich Plasma) therapy to look into although I have no experience with it. Others that have tried it have seen good results and this also works for other illnesses as they are discovering. Such as pancreatitis in cats, severe wound healing in animal limbs etc.

Just know, if you try one thing for a while and it doesn't seem to help, try something else or change what you are doing. It may be the dosing of supplements. Every dog is different and every dog will need different things. What's important is to keep chemicals and toxins of all kinds out of the body. Keep the body moving. Find the correct combination of supplements and physical therapy that keeps your dog moving, and provide a good healthy balanced diet. This will take work on your part to find your dog's best regimen. All commercial pet foods are toxic.

If you will do all of these things, you will find your dog walking pain-free in about 8 weeks depending on the injury or joint issue. Then you continue to build them up and get them really going and getting them back to normal. Yes it is possible. You must work at rehabilitating your dog. In the long run, the cost is less than surgery any vet wants you to jump into right away. Trust me. I have heard vets say "Your dog needs surgery NOW or else" when in fact, that dog didn't. After 6-12 weeks of making dietary changes and adding in supplements along with rehab, the dog was walking much better and pain-free after following everything I have recommended above.

I spoke with someone that had her dog on NSAIDs for 2 years and the dog was still barely moving and having a hard time rising from sitting. That dog's organs were starting to give way I am sure. I got her to get her dog off of NSAIDs after starting CanineActiv, Actiflex for horses in liquid form, and Adequan; the dog is now walking well and pain free with only an occasional flare up. This same dog has severe hip dysplasia. There are almost no hip sockets left. The dog really needs a THR (Total Hip Replacement) surgery. But the dog is doing well even in these extremely severe cases. It's unreal he can walk but he is doing great and off pain medications completely. Never give up hope until you have tried all alternatives before ever considering surgery or euthanasia. Many things can be done and each dog is different, so please if you are still having trouble and have done all the above, get in touch with me. Your case would be considered unique with other options to try. Of course every case is unique in my opinion.

What is P.R.O.M.?

PROM stands for (passive range of motion). This is where your dog is laying down, bearing no weight on the leg and you work the leg by placing your hands on the leg and rotating in a bicycle motion slowly and carefully. Start with 10 repetitions and work up. Doing these repetitively 3 times a day in short intervals will increase muscle mass in your dog's leg. Go to YouTube. There are many videos on how to perform this on your dog. I suggest you watching several different videos to get an idea of what each orthopedic vet or therapist is recommending. Or better yet, ask your dog's therapist to show you how.

Hydrotherapy

Hydrotherapy can be used in the treatment of Osteoarthritis, orthopedic conditions, neurological conditions, muscle, ligament and other soft tissue injuries. Muscle waste begins in approximately 3 days of any injury so to reduce more wasting or re-injury, it is important to rebuild muscle using safe exercise and help rebuild any muscles that have deteriorated. It is better for dogs to swim in warm water since cold water causes constriction of the blood vessels near the skin and restricts the flow of blood therefore making the muscles less efficient.

Hydrotherapy can help with:

- Relief of pain, swelling & stiffness
- Muscle strengthening and maintenance
- Alleviating muscle spasms
- Increased range of motion in joints
- Improved circulation
- Cardiovascular fitness (heart & lungs)
- Increased tissue healing
- Increased speed of recovery

Being in water reduces the heavy load on the limbs and in the back in which helps to reduce pain and re-injury to other joints. Hydrotherapy can also help with nerve regeneration. When the chest area is under water, the lungs must work harder so this increases respiratory breaths therefore increasing oxygen into the blood supply. Using water creates a harder workout therefore rebuilding and healing works much faster. Hydrotherapy can be used for many conditions:

- Obesity
- Joint and soft tissue injury
- Pain and inflammation
- Increasing muscle
- Spinal Injuries
- Muscle Spasms

Hydrotherapy is also considered to be a natural anti-inflammatory through its ability to reduce tissue swelling.

Laser Therapy (also called Low Level Laser or Cold Laser)
Laser therapy works well in combination with other treatments. These lasers used by professionals are usually in a Class IV. This type of laser is deep penetrating and can burn if used incorrectly. This is why only a professionally trained therapist should use them. Class 3b is surface type lasers and do not burn and can be used in a home setting. They do go below the surface but not near as deep as the Class IV. You can buy these in health stores and online stores. The time on it will need to be longer than the Class IV. Usually 15-30 minutes with a Class 3b. You will need to shave the hair in that area to penetrate the skin layers. Laser therapy works well on speeding the healing process on joints and soft tissue injuries. Works well along using other methods of therapies.

PRP
Platelet-rich plasma, or PRP, is derived from blood that is drawn from the patient and run through a special centrifuge, which separates the bloods less dense components from its heavier ones. This process distills a portion of the blood to a platelet concentration level that is much richer than regular blood. At the same time, it helps to remove both red and white blood cells from the platelet rich part of the plasma.

PRP works for cruciate ligament injuries, orthopedic fractures and delayed bone healing, as well as degenerative joint disease of the shoulder, elbow, hip, knee, and ankle. The number of injections per-formed depends upon the severity and type of condition being treated. The use of certain anti-inflammatory drugs is not recommended during PRP therapy as they may diminish the success of the procedure by interfering with the initial inflammatory reaction induced by the platelets. Other therapy is recommended in conjunction with PRP such as laser therapy, hydrotherapy, and acupuncture. This is a low cost procedure.

Hyperbaric Oxygen Chamber Therapy
Hyperbaric oxygen chambers are pressurized tubes where oxygen therapy is delivered. This technique has been used in humans to treat many conditions including air bubbles in blood vessels, decompres-sion sickness ("the bends"), carbon monoxide poisoning, wounds that won't heal, crushing injuries, a skin or bone infection that causes tissue death, snake bites, smoke inhalation, burns, severe anemia, soft tissue injuries as well as joint inflammation and even cancer. HBOT can do so much for many ailments and diseases. It's beyond our scope on the possibilities. Adding a high concentration of oxygen into the blood supply accelerates healing and kills cancer cells. Look for a facility in your area that offers this to pets. The costs are around $135 per treatment depending on what area you live in. The total treatment time is usually 1-2 hours as the pet rests quietly while in the chamber.

There are several supplements for joints I really like to recom-mend especially for moderate to severe cases. Or any dogs having a problem walking, rising etc. That is DC-Y, Actiflex, TRF 150 and CanineActiv. I am sure there are some that are even much better (organic) but these are budget friendly.

Actiflex (equine)
Actiflex is for horses and is stronger. It contains glucosamine that I feel should be in every diet for every dog.
Ingredients: Glucosamine Sulfate, Chondroitin Sulfate, Ester C (Ascorbic Acid), Superoxide Dismutase (SOD), Boswellia Serrata, Hyaluronic Acid, Methylsulfonylmethane (MSM), Perna Canaliculus, Bioperine, Yucca, Purified water, Pina colada flavoring.

1 tsp is approximately:

Glucosamine Sulfate	1,334 mg.
Chondroitin Sulfate	667 mg.
MSM	500 mg.
Ester C (Ascorbic Acid)	167 mg.
Perna Canaliculus	167 mg.
Yucca	25 mg.
Hyaluronic Acid (HA)	21 mg.
Bioperine	17 mg.

Dosage: 1 tsp (5 ml) per 50 lbs. You can give more than this in extreme severe cases for loading dose for several weeks or until you see clear signs of no limping or pain. Usually within 3-5 days you will begin to see change. If not, increase the dosage.

If your dog happens to vomit after giving this, then your dog is probably having a reaction to the MSM or possibly the vitamin C. Some dogs cannot tolerate MSM although uncommon and vitamin C will cause loose stools and diarrhea if given in high amounts with first dose. Just start small and work up.

DC-Y made by MVP (equine)

This is an all anti-inflammatory herb mix. It comes in a meal. A meal is not a fine powder but a mix of powder and tiny pieces of herbs. Kind of like what we may use in our kitchen spices. Small particles. Easy to mix in with wet foods. It has an apple flavoring so it doesn't smell like greens powders. Anti-inflammatory herbs will reduce inflammation in the body including joints, soft tissues and any organ that is inflamed. As you know, anytime the body has a disease, ill or injury, there will be inflammation. So if your dog has an infection in a wound or sore, that inflammation travels throughout the entire body and aggravates joints and other parts of the body. So one illness can cause a flare up in another. This is why it is important to use these anti-inflammatories to conquer illness, disease and joint issues.

DC-Y contains Devil's Claw, Yucca, Grape Seed Meal, Boswellia, Cat's Claw, Turmeric, Fever Few, and White Willow Bark...in that order. Also Alfalfa meal. It contains natural and artificial flavors (apple).

Approximate dosing for dogs:
Small dogs: 1/4-1/2 tsp
Medium dogs: 1/2-1 tsp
Large dogs: 1 tsp -1 1/2 tsp
Giant dogs: 2 tsp

*If your dog has leukemia, do not give since this contains Cat's Claw.
If your dog has low blood pressure, Cat's Claw may lower blood
pressure even more.*

If you would like an organic version of anti-inflammatories, you can
gather these ingredients online and purchase organic powders then
combine. Choose Grape Seed Extract wisely. No skin or meat. Only
seeds from grapes. Make sure it says 100% grape seed. Grape seed
extract has terrific healing abilities for many diseases including
cancer. You want to add flavor? You can find organic apple or
blueberry powders as well.
I plan to buy organic powders and make my own. Well worth the
money and allowing me to not worry about what's going in the body.
If you want organic powders and need help in finding them, just
contact me through one of my websites/email and I will be glad to
help you.

List to purchase for a good combo in **organic:**
Yucca
Devil's Claw
Grape Seed Extract (seeds only)
Boswellia
Turmeric
Rosehips (tart flavor)
Blueberry powder

You will measure and mix then add to wet foods daily. You can split
it into two meals if you like. Use some and put into capsules for yourself. Dosage will be the same as the DC-Y. I prefer the organic myself and this will be what I will be doing.

*Keep the amounts of Yucca lower as a higher dose has been known
to cause bloat in horses and could cause bloat in larger dogs. It's best*

to discontinue yucca for awhile after about 3 months of use. Not for long term use without interruptions in dosing.

CanineActiv

CanineActiv relieves pain and inflammation while promoting healthy, natural healing and repair of damaged tissue for dogs of any breed. CanineActiv Safe Pain Relief contains the anti-inflammatory ingredient, Alpha-GEE®, a unique compound made of naturally occurring amino acids found in natural sources and endogenous to a dog's body. They are part of a dog's normal healing process and CanineActiv helps optimize restoration of healthy mobility.

Ingredients:
Alpha-GEE/Amino Acids, Boswellia Serrata/BOSWELLIA, Glycyrrhiza Glabra/Licorice Root, Harpagophytum/Devils Claw, Curmuma longa/Curcumin-Turmeric, Medicago sativa/Alfalfa, Tanacetum parthenium/Feverfew, Yucca schidigera/YUCCA
Use to relieve pain and inflammation and help increase mobility. Can be used as a preventative before activity.

Note: CanineActiv can produce a false-positive test in blood work causing liver enzymes to be higher. If your dog has liver issues already, please discontinue using this at least 48 hours before blood work. If your dog has heart disease, do not give as Licorice Root can cause more harm.

Do not take with or add water to this. Can add whole capsule into food or treat or open capsule and sprinkle onto moist/wet foods.

TRF 150

TRF 150™ provides nutritional support for healthy joint function, repair, and relief of occasional inflammation. These products feature Cyplexinol™ PRO, a bone derived protein/collagen complex containing Bone Morphogenetic Proteins (BMPs) and key growth factors naturally contained in bones. This ingredient helps to support pathways involved in normal bone remodeling, and the proper repair and regeneration of cartilage, thereby supporting good bone health and joint integrity.

Tissue Regeneration Factor (TRF) is an ideal first line of defense for any stage of osteoporosis, broken or fractured bones, and for any condition in need of joint or cartilage repair.

- Stimulates new bone and cartilage formation
- Anti inflammatory
- Can be taken with or without meals

TRF is available in 150 mg and 350 mg doses. Use TRF 350™ when higher dosages are desired for more serious bone and cartilage support or larger dogs.

Note: I started Sydney on TRF 150 for her ACL tear and I have seen some nice results. I really like this supplement.

Anti-inflammatory herbs are:
Devil's Claw
Yucca Root
Grape Seed Extract (no skins or meat-seeds only and organic)
Fever Few
Cat's Claw
Turmeric
Boswellia
Organic Alfalfa
Ginger
Meadowsweet

Some supplements good for joints:
Camu Camu/Rosehips/Amla
Fish oil (high quality)
Glucosamine
Chondroitin
Cetyl-Myristoleate
Bromelain
Green Lipped Mussel
MSM
Hyaluronic Acid (HA)
Mushroom Blends

Note: Check out my new book called "Canine Arthritis & Joint Pain: Healing Naturally". It covers this chapter and more.

Stay away from Inactive type ingredients such as:

Sodium benzoate	Propylene glycol	Lecithin (soy)	Polyethylene glycol (PEG)
Sucralose	Canola oil	Corn Starch	Sorbitol or Mannitol
Safflower Oil	Vegetable or corn oil	Xanthan Gum	Carrageenan
Citric Acid (corn based)	Artificial Flavorings	Soybean protein isolate	Benzoic Acid
Rosemary Extract	Potassium Sorbate	FD&C Red #40 (all food colors avoid)	Caramel Color
Stearic acid	Gelatin (corn carrier)	Dicalcium phosphate	Dextrose
Magnesium Stearate	Silicon dioxide	Soy	Maltodextrin (corn based)
Titanium Dioxide	Sorbic acid (a preservative)	Brown Rice Syrup	Hydrolyzed Vegetable Protein

These are a small portion to avoid but some of your main ones to watch out for. I find that Magnesium Stearate as well as Silicon dioxide is in many things. Try to avoid if you can although not always possible under certain circumstances.

Avoid tablets (full of junk ingredients) and softgels (will not dissolve in dogs short intestinal tracts). Use powders, capsules or liquid extracts that contain no preservatives or alcohol. You will find vegetable glycerin in place of alcohol. As I said it takes work to avoid junk ingredients but try the best you can. If you can reduce most of the bad ingredients, then you are cutting down on what the body must try to filter out and not absorb into the body causing more issues.

Inflammation is the root cause of nearly every disease

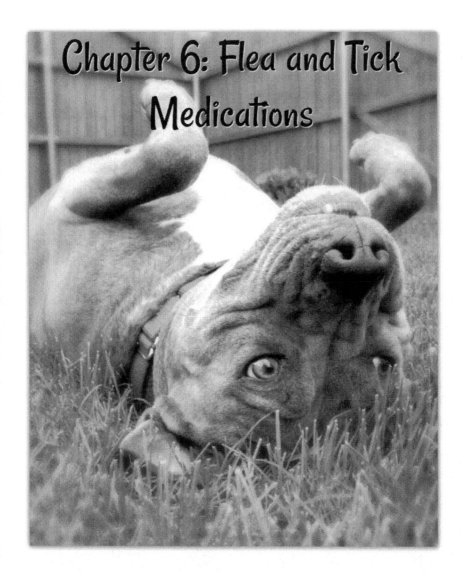

Chapter 6: Flea and Tick Medications

Chapter 6
Flea and Tick Medications

Pet Parents purchase toxic chemicals intended to kill fleas and ticks. These include collars, sprays, dusts and more. Other Pet Parents take their pets to vets to be dipped in chemicals. Same for groomers that dip dogs. Many consumers probably assume that the products used by both parties have been tested and deemed safe. After all, how could the FDA let deadly poisons be sold on store shelves? Well that's a loaded question.

Spot-On Pesticides such as Frontline Plus, Sentinel, Comfortis, Trifexis, Assurity, Revolution, PetArmor, Bravecto, Hartz, Sergeants, NexGuard, K9 Advantix II, Biospot and Advantage just to name a few, can trigger adverse reactions in dogs and cats, shorten life spans, cause terminal illness, and premature death.

The active ingredients in these solutions include chemicals such as imidacloprid, fipronil, permethrin, methoprene, and pyriproxyfen, all of which have caused serious health problems in animals. Even some of the inactive ingredients can be hazardous to your pet. Other forms of flea control powders (including carpet powders), collars and sprays are no less dangerous to you or your pets.

These products are considered pesticides. Avoid these pesticides for safer alternatives.

Immediate effects of pesticide overdose include vomiting, diarrhea, trembling, seizures, and respiratory problems. If your dog or cat shows any of these symptoms after the application of a pesticide, immediately wash the product off and seek immediate emergency veterinary care.

Products containing cyphenothrin and permethrin were especially problematic for small dogs.

Veterinarians have seen a huge increase in the rate of liver disease, nervous system disorders, cancers, seizures, diabetes, renal failure and other diseases. These popular anti-flea and anti-tick medications are extremely toxic to the liver.

Any dogs under 12 lbs should not use any flea and tick medications or topicals ever. And use extra caution with Essential oils as well.

*The EPA issued an advisory a couple years ago about spot-on products after receiving over **44,000 reports of adverse reactions, including 600 deaths. Don't be another statistic.***

NEVER give your dog Spinosad and Ivermectin at the same time.

Effects are DEADLY!!

Please err on the side of caution and don't use these (or any OTC) toxic flea treatments on your pets. Feel free to email, phone or write the FDA and tell the chemical and pharmaceutical companies that we REFUSE to POISON our pets in order to kill fleas.

You can try different non-toxic products on the market. They are out there and I have found a few for you. While some may work better than others so depending on your situation, as to which one may work best or in combination. Just keep searching for the one that works best for you. It may take going through a couple before you do find that combination.

Some of the Safe Products to try are:
Food Grade Diatomaceous Earth (DE) (Yard and internal dosing)
Triple Sure
PetSafe Pure Red Cedar Insect Repellent Granules
Mercola Flea and Tick Defense
FLEA AND TICK SPRAY (sold at Hare Today)
Sentry Natural Defense Natural Flea & Tick Squeeze-On for Dogs
Wondercide EVOLV: Natural Flea & Tick Control
Ticked Off!
Green Pet Fleaze-Off Wipes
Petzlife
TickZ - Controls Ticks and other biting insects
Alzoo Natural Flea & Tick Spot On Dog Repellent
Fleabusters Rx for Fleas Plus Powder
No More Ticks
Pet Protector Disc
Apple Cider Vinegar
Ambertick

For lawns:
The Orcon Flea Destroyer (7 million) (FD-C7M)
CedarCide Pco Choice Organic Yard Pest Control
Food Grade Diatomaceous Earth (DE)
Wondercide

117

It may be best to use several different types of things like Diatomaceous Earth for yard, the safe products above and be vigilant about where your dog roams and trying to keep the yard contained with a heavily treated perimeter.

You can also try your hand at homemade remedies:

Colloidal Silver
Fleas: Use as a flea spray- saturate the fleas with colloidal silver daily until gone.

How many sprays or droppers = 1 teaspoon
50 vertical sprays = 1 teaspoon (5 ml)
30 fine mist sprays = 1 teaspoon (5 ml)
6 (2 oz/60 ml) droppers = 1 teaspoon (5 ml)
5 (4 oz/120 ml) droppers = 1 teaspoon (5 ml)
5 (8 oz/240 ml) droppers = 1 teaspoon (5 ml)
1 teaspoon=5 cc
2 teaspoons = 10cc

Apple Cider Vinegar (raw, "Mother")
Internal Dosage:
0-25 lbs: 1 teaspoon
25-50 lbs: 2 teaspoon
50-75 lbs: 1 TBSP
75+ lbs: 1 1/2-2 TBSP

External:
Sponge on ACV diluted with equal amounts of warm water. All fleas drown in soapy water and the ACV rinse makes the skin too acidic for a re-infestation. If you are worried about picking up fleas when you take your dog away from home, keep some ACV in a spray bottle, and spray your dog before you leave home, and when you get back. Take some with you and keep it in the car, just in case you need it any time. ACV normalizes the pH levels of the skin, makes your dog unpalatable to even the nastiest of bacteria.
Don't give up in getting away from these deadly medications of all kinds. Try these natural products, many use essential oils and are

diluted so that they will not cause harm to your dog. But always watch your pets when applying something new. Also wash your hands once you use anything. No need to share it everywhere else. You could touch a baby and it have a reaction or in your eyes. Always wash your hands after handling anything whether it is safe or not. And be very careful using on small dogs or puppies. Even the natural products can cause serious reactions as well.

Cedar Oil is a great product to use. You can dilute it with coconut oils and apply to your pet's coat. It works well. The Health Ranger (Mike Adams) is working on a pet product as I write this that contains cedar oil.

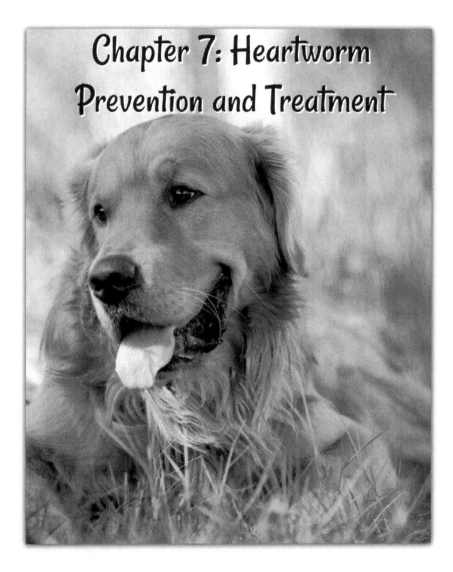
Chapter 7: Heartworm Prevention and Treatment

Chapter 7
Heartworm Treatment and Prevention

It is important to understand that heartworm infections are not detectable until about six months after a dog has been bitten by a heartworm-infected mosquito. (This is why it's not possible to have a heartworm test performed monthly and give the preventative only if an infection is found.) Blood tests generally will not detect heartworms in a dog until the larvae have matured into an adult worm, which takes about six months following initial infection. Symptoms, such as coughing, lethargy and difficulty breathing, will not show up until the infection is advanced. Coughing will be your first symptom in the earlier stages.

Once heartworm infection has been confirmed, additional tests should be done to try to determine how extensive the infestation is. Radiographs can reveal inflammation and damage to the arteries and the heart, and blood tests will show whether the liver and kidneys have been affected.

Heartworm infection is divided into four or five stages (depending on the model used), based on the severity of the infestation and the age and health of the dog.

- Stage 1 (mild) consists of young, healthy dogs with no symptoms and minimal changes evident on x-rays.

- Stage 2 (moderate) infection will show heartworm disease that is evident on x-rays, but symptoms are minimal, mostly coughing.

- Stage 3 is a severe infection, with weight loss, coughing, difficulty breathing, more damage visible on x-rays, along with liver and/or kidney damage.

- Stage 4 and 5 are considered critical, with the dog often collapsing in shock. These dogs will not survive ordinary heartworm treatment, and must have the worms surgically removed if they are to have any hope of survival.

I recommend using all-natural products and no chemicals to treat a heartworm positive dog. Natural treatments are safer and work just as well as medications. I have a list on my **Holistic and Organix Pet Shoppe** website. Just know, NO medication or natural supplement PREVENTS heartworm. These do not prevent. They kill after being infected. The best thing you can do is keep a strong immune system and test your dog every 6-12 months.

If you elect to use the chemicals using the slow-kill method (no Immiticide), then I recommend giving normal doses of Heartgard Plus (Ivermectin) monthly along with pulsed Doxycycline. Some studies show that you can give Heartgard every 15 days for 6 months to treat heartworm positive dogs.

(Note that a dog may test positive for up to six months after the worms are all gone).

Remember that anything that increases your dog's heart rate increases the risk as long as your dog is infected with heartworms.

Ivermectin is not recommended for dogs with the MDR1 gene mutation that causes sensitivity to Ivermectin.

Options for pulsing Doxycycline:

Give Doxycycline for one month (one month on, two months off, one month on.) Dosage may be repeated 6 months later - Doxy for one month).
Dosage of Doxycycline can be cut in half if the dog cannot tolerate a higher dose. Giving it with food can help prevent digestive upset.

Here are the supporting details on Wolbachia and Doxycycline:
Research has led to the discovery of a parasite called Wolbachia that lives symbiotically inside heartworms. Studies indicate that this parasite contributes to the adverse effects of both heartworm infection and heartworm treatment, including inflammation, embolism and allergic reaction.

Treatment with Doxycycline to kill the Wolbachia parasite weakens the heartworms and makes them unable to reproduce, lessens their adverse effects on the body and greatly reduces the chance of adverse reaction during heartworm treatment.

Studies published in late 2008 clearly indicate that treatment with a combination of Ivermectin and daily Doxycycline given intermittently will sterilize the heartworms, prevent the dog from being infectious to other dogs (via mosquitoes), speed up the death of the worms prior to (or in place of) Immiticide treatment, limit inflammation and damage caused by the worms' presence, and reduce the chance of serious adverse reaction from Immiticide treatment.

All of these work best when the two drugs are used together than when either is given alone.

TIP: Start the Doxycycline one month before starting the Heartgard to lessen any reactions to the Heartgard that may cause the dog to throw a worm.

"Treatment with Ivermectin combined with Doxycycline resulted in a significantly faster decrease of circulating microfilariae and higher adulticidal [killed more adult heartworms] activity compared with either Ivermectin or Doxycycline alone. . . . Results indicate that the combination of these two drugs causes adult worm death."

Any dog that is currently infected with heartworms should be treated with Doxycycline. All dogs except those with multi-drug sensitivity should also be given a regular monthly dose of Heartgard (Ivermectin) every month until heartworms are gone.

A laboratory study done on Wolbachia showed that intermittent treatment with antibiotics was more effective in depleting Wolbachia than continuous treatment.

Immiticide Injections are NOT recommended..ever!

Affected Breeds of the MDR1 Gene

The University Of Washington states: Approximately three of every four Collies in the United States have the mutant MDR1 gene. The frequency is about the same in France and Australia, so it is likely that most Collies worldwide have the mutation. The MDR1 mutation has also been found in Shetland Sheepdogs (Shelties). Australian Shepherds, Old English Sheepdogs, English Shepherds, German Shepherds, Long-haired Whippets, Silken Windhounds, and a variety of mixed breed dogs.

The only way to know if an individual dog has the mutant MDR1 gene is to have the dog tested. As more dogs are tested, more breeds will probably be added to the list of affected breeds.

Breeds affected by the MDR1 mutation (frequency %)

Breed		Approximate Frequency	
Australian Shepherd	50%	Long-haired Whippet	65 %
Australian Shepherd, Mini	50%	McNab	30 %
Border Collie	< 5%	Mixed Breed	5 %
Collie	70 %	Old English Sheepdog	5 %
English Shepherd	15 %	Shetland Sheepdog	15 %
German Shepherd	10 %	Silken Windhound	30 %
Herding Breed Cross	10 %		

They also offer the MDR1 Test for a small fee. Well worth the life of your dog.

Dosing for Doxycycline:

These are approximate dosing suggestions so **please check with your vet before giving medications prescribed for the correct dosage.**

This should be given for 4 weeks. Wait 1-2 months and repeat this step. Twice should be plenty.

Quick Guide dosage directions (100mg Doxycycline):
10-20 lbs: 1/2 tab twice a day
20-30 lbs: 1 tab twice a day
31-40 lbs: 1 tab twice a day
41-50 lbs: 1 1/2 tab twice a day
51-60 lbs: 2 tabs twice a day
61-70 lbs: 2 - 3 tabs twice a day
71-80 lbs: 3 - 4 tabs twice a day
81-90 lbs: 3 1/2 - 4 1/2 tabs twice a day
91-100 lbs: 5 tabs twice a day

If your dog is safe from not having the MDR1 gene, you can purchase straight Ivermectin from a feed store and give it monthly at the same dosage. (Check with your vet on dosage). Please watch the dog for the first 12 hours very closely up to 72 hours after the dosage is given. Your dog could have a reaction to it so be prepared if it does. This is uncommon but can happen so always be prepared for an emergency. My dog did and it was a severe reaction and was very close to dying.

**Most feed stores/vet supply houses that carry this can help you with dosage as well.

Have your dog tested every 6 months till she/he is clear and tests are negative. It can take approximately 9-18 months to become negative according to how badly the dog was infected.
It's not unusual for the microfilaria to be seen in the blood for well up to a year after killing the adult heartworms. The microfilaria cannot turn into adult heartworms without being sucked up by a mosquito and going through the 4th stage and being re-injected into a dog. While stepping up the post-treatment with a higher dosage of Heartgard and given every 2 weeks along with using a Heartworm Nosode. In 3 months, this should be cleared and test is negative. Just use caution!

** I DO NOT recommend having the injections done (Immiticide treatment) EVER, since this can cause serious with sometimes-deadly reactions. Only under severe cases of heartworm would I recommend surgery AND it may be the only option for removal!

When using the Immiticide injection treatment, the dog needs to be crated for months. Absolutely no activity, no running, playing etc. With the slow kill, they can continue their normal activities just as long as you don't get the heart rate up too much. However they are able to go to the potty off leash and do not have to be crated as they would have to be when giving the deadly injections unless you have a super hyper dog. Always keep an eye on the dog right after giving doses for at least 72 hours with the first 12 hours being the most crucial time since reactions are possible with every dog in every case.

There are quite a few natural remedies out there that are much better. All of these have a 75% or higher success rate. You can try them and if they still don't kill out the worms, slow kill (Heartgard and Doxy) is your best way to go. Once you have completed the treatment, your dog will highly benefit from supplements recommended for heart disease. For the natural supplements for heartworm treatment and prevention or for heart disease, please contact me and I will provide you with this information or see chapter 7.

Natural Remedies to Prevent Heartworm
There is a homeopathic nosode that is made from heartworm larvae that is used commonly by holistic veterinarians as a preventive to avoid the drug side effects. However, many question its effectiveness, though some people who use the nosode (apparently successfully) with animals in heartworm endemic areas. I use this for my 5 dogs and all have remained heartworm negative.

Dosing for the nosode is as follows: 30C potency given once a week. These can be given to dogs that are heartworm positive in a higher dose.
As I had mentioned about using homeopathic remedies earlier in this book, this is one time I overlook the "why I don't use them" and use them. Heartworms are nothing to play around with so give this once a week using this nosode. Add (3-5) pellets into a 4 ounce glass bottle using filtered water, shake vigorously until dissolved, and then squirt into your dog's mouth one full syringe. Store in frig for 2 weeks. You can also put directly into the mouth to dissolve or add into foods.

Warning: Doxycycline is a very powerful antibiotic and must be given with food. Doxycycline can cause severe diarrhea (blood also) and vomiting even after first dose. If this happens, stop Doxycycline and call vet immediately. It has caused death under these circumstances. Do not give to ill dogs or weakened immune systems. Give Probiotics and digestive enzymes when using Doxycycline.

See *HolisticAndOrganixPetShoppe.com* for more information on all-natural treatment and remedies.

For use of the homeopathic heartworm nosode for **prevention**:
- 3 pellets for small dogs a week
- 4 pellets for medium dogs a week

- 5 pellets for large dogs a week

 Don't forget; have your dog tested every 6 months until all negative results.

There are many all natural treatments and preventions out there so go to my website for an up-to-date list of all your options. Just please avoid those injections pushed by vets that are truly very dangerous and toxic if your dog ever becomes heartworm positive. The odds of a raw fed healthy dog becoming heartworm positive are next to nonexistent. Mosquito's feed on weakened immune systems. Keep your dogs healthy and strong by following this book of recommendations.

Herbs for killing heartworms but use under the guidance of a holistic vet:

- Parsley
- Wormwood
- Black Walnut Hull
- Hops
- Grapefruit Seed Extract
- Sorrel
- Cloves
- Neem
- Garlic

Petwellbeing.com has a formula that is made without the Black Walnut and Wormwood. Contact them on the precautions. May be safer to use but anytime a dog has heartworms, you should closely monitor your dog for the first 12-72 hours after dosing with anything. Stay on the side of caution but this is fairly simple to remedy your dog using natural products without using toxic chemicals or medications. You can even speak with the makers of these herbal mixes and they can guide you and will be happy to do so.

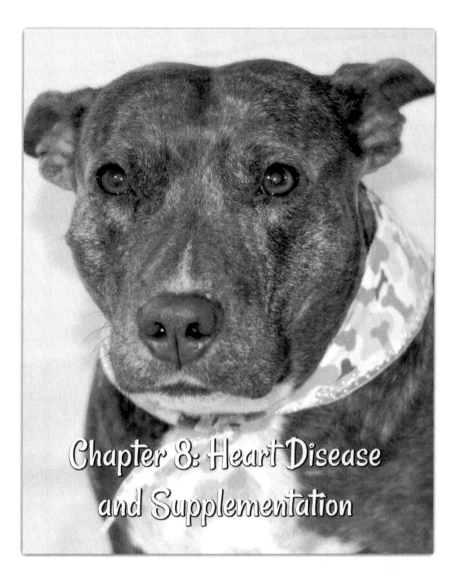

Chapter 8: Heart Disease and Supplementation

Chapter 8
Heart Disease and Supplementation

If your dog is getting into his/her senior years or has had heartworms now or in the past, you need to read this chapter so you will know how to help prevent heart disease in your dog.

If you wait too long and your dog shows signs of heart disease like lethargy, wheezing, coughing or has a hard time walking or running, it's often too late to save your beloved dog for living a longer life, but with supplements you can help extend his/her life and help them to be comfortable throughout their lasting years and possibly extend their life further.

If your vet suspects heart disease, he/she will usually want x-rays, EKG or cardiac ultrasound. Many times he/she will find the heart enlarged, possibly fluid in the lungs. Your vet will also listen with a stethoscope for missed or skipped heartbeats causing a heart murmur.

Some breeds are predisposed to heart conditions, including New Foundlands, Cavalier King Charles Spaniel, Great Danes and Dobermans. But no dog is excluded. Much depends on the breeding line, the diet and overall care of the dog. Dogs with heart disease will be lacking sufficient nutrients.

Heart murmurs are ranked on a scale from 1 to 6, where 1 is considered mild and 6 is the worst case.

These symptoms are what to look for in heart disease:

- Abdominal distention
- Exercise intolerance
- Lethargy/weakness
- Coughing/Gagging
- Breathing difficulty
- Bluish skin/gums
- Sleeping more
- Loss of appetite
- Rapid weight loss

There is a blood test for early detection in heart disease. It's called the ProBNP test. (B-type Natriuretic Peptide) This test measures the peptide hormone that the heart releases. This only shows up when the heart is under pressure or working harder than it should be. This test can prepare you for the future to help your dog's heart function better and last longer without causing more stress. You can have this done at any age but in larger breeds, I would start around 4-5 years of age and check it either yearly or every other year depending on dog, but can be done as often as necessary.

Probiotics and Digestive enzymes are important. The goal here is to make the immune system strong and rebuild/repair muscles, liver etc. If you have a healthy gut, you will have a healthier body. Diet plays an extremely important roll. A homemade diet (raw preferably) is your best diet. **Do not feed commercial pet foods. Homemade only but make sure you have all the correct supplements for a homemade diet.** Do not feed anything with salt in it. Provide fresh filtered multi-stage chlorine and fluoride-free water at all times.

If your dog is on medications, add milk thistle to the diet to help filter the liver.

If your pet is suffering from a heart condition, you may want to try these vitamins and herbs. It has been documented that these have shown an improvement in heart conditions, and even eliminating medications or stopping them altogether.

For **prevention** of heart disease, you can give these supplements (several or all):

- Ubiquinol/COQ10
- L-Arginine
- Organic Hawthorn powder
- Taurine (try to find one not sourced from China because most are or feed raw heart meat)
- Propionyl-L-Carnitine
- Fulvic/Humic Acid
- Organic Astragalus powder
- D-Ribose (lower amounts)

I myself had a dog suffering from a heart murmur and with these supplements; I was able to stop all coughing and stopped all medications. Give it a few weeks to see if coughing subsides. Another dog with more severe symptoms was treated using all of these below and the coughing was cut in half.

This is a complete list of all supplements that will work for heart disease if your dog has already been **diagnosed**:

- Ubiquinol/COQ10
- Pycnogenol or Pine Bark Extract
- L-Arginine
- Organic Hawthorn powder
- Taurine (try to find one not sourced from China because most are or feed raw heart meat)
- L-Carnitine
- D-Ribose
- Magnesium Orotate (heart, one of the best absorbing)
- Vitamin C (ester C-Magnesium Ascorbate) or better yet - Camu Camu or Rosehips)
- Vitamin E (Dry E Succinate) (soy free)
- Fish Oil (sardine/anchovy or squid)
- Organic Turmeric
- Organic Dandelion Leaf
- Fulvic/Humic Acid

These are best when split into 2 doses per day. Do not throw all of these into one meal and not expect reactions. In other words, add two supplements into wet foods daily for 7 days, if no reaction (diarrhea, vomiting) then add 2-3 more into diet, give for 5-7 days then add a couple more and so on. Work up to getting all of these in the diet. It's a lot I know but, do this and see what happens. If your dog isn't better within 4 weeks, you can choose to cut back on them. But I would continue use as long as your dog is alive. You may even be able to stop all medications once on these.

Ubiquinol/COQ10
Ubiquinol is better but COQ10 is acceptable as well.

Ubiquinol Dosage:
Small dogs: 50mg per day
Medium dogs: 100mg per day
Large dogs: 100mg twice per day
Giant dogs: 100-200mg twice per day

COQ10 Dosage:
Small dogs: 100 - 200mg daily
Medium dogs: 200 - 300mg daily
Large dogs: 300 - 400mg daily
Giant dogs: 400 - 500mg daily

Pycnogenol or Pine Bark Extract
Dosage: 1-2 mg per lb of body weight.

L-Arginine
Dosage:
Small dogs: 250mg
Medium dogs: 500mg
Large dogs: 750mg
Giant dogs: 1000mg
You can give up to 100mg per lb. daily.

Organic Hawthorn powder
Dosage:
Small dogs: 1/4 tsp
Medium dogs: 3/4 tsp
Large dogs: 1 tsp
Giant dogs: 1 1/2 tsp

Taurine (Also good for epilepsy. Helps heart muscle to contract.)
Dosage:
Small dogs: 250mg
Medium dogs: 500mg
Large dogs: 750mg
B- Complex vitamins work well with Taurine.

L-Carnitine
Dosage:
Small dogs: 250mg
Medium dogs: 500mg
Large dogs: 750mg
Giant dogs: 1000mg

D-Ribose
Dosage:
Small dogs: 500 mg
Medium dogs: 1000 mg
Large dogs: 1500 mg
Giant dogs: 2000 mg
You can give higher amounts in severe cases.

Magnesium Orotate (heart, one of the best absorbing)
Dosage:
Small dogs: 10mg
Medium dogs: 20mg
Large dogs: 50mg
Giant dogs: 75mg
Or when using powder 1/8 teaspoon up to 1/2 teaspoon depending on size of dog.

Astragalus *(Astragalus membranaceous)*
Immunostimulant, antiviral, anti-inflammatory, hypothyroid (mildly depresses thyroid function), hypotensive, digestive tonic. Works on immune systems, lungs, liver, **heart**, kidneys, thyroid, and digestive tract.
Astragalus is used for strengthening the body against viral infections of the respiratory and heart. Astragalus can be used for early treatment of a variety of respiratory infections, including kennel cough (Bordetella bronchiseptica). Astragalus helps to raise white blood cell counts and also boosts the body's immune system. Astragalus may be useful for helping the body protect itself and speed recovery from the damages of long term steroid medications. Astragalus is also useful in early stages of kidney infection and/or renal failure. Astragalus is non-toxic in any dosages. Buy organic.

Powder
Dosage:
Small dogs: 1/4 tsp
Medium dogs: 3/4 tsp
Large dogs: 1 tsp
Giant dogs: 1 1/2 tsp

Vitamin C - (Buffered/Ester C-*Magnesium Ascorbate*) or Camu
Camu or Rosehips)
Dosage:
Adjust accordingly but a good place to start or work towards.
Small dogs: 500mg - 1500mg
Medium/Large dogs: 1000mg - 3000mg
Giant dogs: 2000mg - 4000mg

Powder
Dosage:
Small dogs: 1/4 tsp
Medium dogs: 3/4 tsp
Large dogs: 1 tsp
Giant dogs: 1 1/2 tsp

Vitamin E (Dry E Succinate) (soy free):
Dosage:
Small dogs: 200IU
Medium dogs: 300IU
Large dogs: 400IU
Giant dogs: 600IU

Fish Oil (Sardine/Anchovy or Squid):
Dosage:
Small dogs: 500 - 750mg
Medium dogs: 1000 - 1250mg
Large dogs: 1500 - 1750mg
Giant dogs: 2000 - 2250mg

Organic Turmeric:
This herb is strong flavored and smells with a bright orange color.
And it even will stain. May cause stomach upset for sensitive
tummies. Terrific for all ailments and diseases except kidney stones.
It is important to note that turmeric is a binding agent and a good
remedy for diarrhea as well. It can cause constipation as well as
dehydration so be sure your dog drinks plenty of water when using it.
Turmeric works for most all illness including, joints, heart, cancer etc.
It's a great additive for any ailment and for preventing future illness.

Dosage:
Small dogs: 250mgMedium dogs: 350mg
Large dogs: 500mg
Giant dogs: 750mg
This can be adjusted up or down.

Powder
Dosage:
Small dogs: 1/4 tsp
Medium dogs: 3/4 tsp
Large dogs: 1 tsp
Giant dogs: 1 1/2 tsp

You can purchase capsules and slide into foods if possible or buy smaller (size 0) empty capsules and fill them yourself. Standard capsules are size 00. They go as small as size 4. You can buy them on Amazon, eBay etc.

*Turmeric should not be given to dogs prone to kidney stones. Turmeric isn't supposed to be given with blood thinners. Turmeric should not be combined with drugs that reduce stomach acid (Pepsid, Zantac etc), as the body will actually increase its production of stomach acid, and thus, lead to nausea, stomach pain, bloating, and esophagus damage.

Organic Dandelion Leaf Powder (Diuretic)
Dosage:
Capsules-up to 250 mg a day

Powder
Dosage:
Small dogs: 1/4 tsp
Medium dogs: 3/4 tsp
Large dogs: 1 tsp
Giant dogs: 1 1/2 tsp

Fulvic/Humic Acid
Many pet parents wonder if their pets will be getting "too many minerals" if they are giving other products that also contain minerals such

as a Calcium supplement. The answer is no because Fulvic is extracted from plant material – not rocks or clay. When plant-derived Fulvic enters the system, it is immediately recognized as one of nature's essential substances. It triggers the proper metabolic responses that utilize the minerals where they're needed, discarding those that are not needed. It is impossible for plant-derived minerals to build up in the tissues. Depending on the severity of health issues, you can give higher amounts. Fulvic/Humic Acid detoxifies the body of heavy metals, toxins, and pollutants, increases oxygen absorption in blood, enhances healing, repair, and rejuvenation of the cells - energizes cells, repairs and detoxifies the thyroid.

Do not give alongside medications nor mix with fruit juices. Wait 2 hours in-between.

Approximate Dosing:
Small dogs: 1 teaspoon
Medium dogs: 2 teaspoons
Large dogs: 1 TBSP

Potassium may be needed
Potassium needs may be increased, if you are giving digoxin or diuretics, or decreased if you are treating with ACE inhibitors such as Enalapril, or with spironolactone. Monitor blood potassium levels and make adjustments as needed. Check with your vet before adding any potassium supplements. If you feed a raw diet or are giving Dandelion Leaf, it is probably not needed.

Note that many prescription cardiac diets are high in potassium, which may be inappropriate depending on the medications being used. Some prescription diets are also low in protein, which is always inappropriate for dogs with heart disease. If you are feeding a prescription diet for heart disease, you can improve the quality of the diet by switching to high-protein animal-source foods such as meat, eggs and some dairy (raw goats milk, Kefir), but be careful not to add foods that are high in sodium. For example: Look for low sodium Sardines in water. Avoid Salmon as it is high in sodium. Note that prescription diets are **not** recommended. This can be maintained by a homemade diet (raw or cooked) best. (See Chapter 3)

While this seems like a TON of supplements, **it is**. But these are all known to help the heart. It is **not** recommended to use only one or two. Pick at least 5-10 of these and use them daily for moderate - severe cases. Combinations work much better than single ingredients. You can skip a day or two weekly for the system to have a break. Usually for the first 2-4 weeks , don't skip unless an issue arises. Like I mentioned, I have used them all and at one time and had really good results. Start out with a couple for about 5 days and in lower amounts, if no loose stools or diarrhea, vomiting or loss of appetite, work up to full dose then add two more into the daily diet. If all goes well, in 3-5 days, add in two more. Work your way up to all of the ones you plan on adding. Never throw all of them in at one time on day one with full dose and not expect something to happen. You may obtain cannon butt (diarrhea) if you do. Poop always plays a crucial role in knowing where your dog is at in his diet, or anything going into the body. Vitamin C (all ascorbates) will cause diarrhea or loose stools in higher doses. This is not a problem. Just back off of the amount you gave until no more diarrhea. Maybe give some 100% organic pumpkin to help with the symptoms of diarrhea. Organic diets for a diseased heart will help improve your dog's health as well.

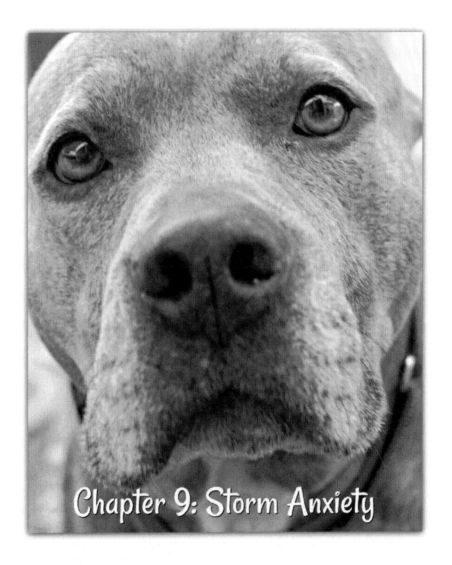

Chapter 9: Storm Anxiety

Chapter 9
Storm Anxiety

Dogs suffer from anxiety caused by different things - loud noise, strangers, children, being alone, car rides, and storms.

It is important to remember that behavior is transferable from one dog to another. If I had encouraged the unbalanced behavior of who behaved in an unbalanced way, the behavior of the other dogs would have become unstable also. **It is also transferable from human to dog.**

Some dogs can sense an earthquake minutes before we feel any sign ourselves. A dog's sensitivity to environmental changes (barometric pressure changes, noise, visual, electrical energy etc.) varies from one dog to another. Some dogs can find environmental changes bothersome or even painful.

Dogs read our body language and sense tension in your voice. They know how you are feeling and sense your stress.

If your dog normally paces or runs around feeling anxious, stop your dog right away! One of the worst things to do is to allow a dog to run around or pace. At this point the dog is driven by fear and does not know where to go or what to do to feel safe. It is really important (once again) that the dog's pet parent takes the leadership role and shows the dog what it should do. If your dog is crate trained, put him/her in their crate. They want guidance at that time - crating them tells them were to be and provides them with a safe haven. Don't baby talk, pat them or worry. Just treat this as normal.

Some phobic dogs will seek out dark, quiet corners on their own where they can calm themselves, so consider providing a dark room, a closet, or space under a table or desk for a frightened pet. The goal is to provide your dog a secure spot that helps him calm himself. Most dogs will find this spot every time fear strikes. Let them stay there and provide them with one of your pieces of clothing for security.

Don't feel stressed or tension within yourself. Your dog will sense this and it will increase his/her emotions. This is all about changing your dog's connection with thunderstorms and your bad habits of supporting and enabling psychological trauma with emotion. Keep the pitch of your voice low as well.
Most dogs that are suffering from social anxiety have this behavioral problem because they have not been properly trained to socialize with other pups and humans.

To desensitize your dog from having "panic attacks" around other dogs or people, for example, slowly introduce a dog (preferably a calm one) or human to your dog, one at a time. Do not attempt to introduce a lot of dogs and/or people to your dog all at once. You will only scare and stress your dog out! This could cause fear biting. You certainly don't want that to happen. Do this once or twice a week at least to help them adjust to people and other pets.

This may take time but continue to reinforce this positive and secure behavior.

You may try soft music for your dog or drown out outside noises with white noise. Try playing with your dog to get his/her mind off of what is really going on. This will take his mind off what's going on outside and can help calm his anxiety as well. It is also helpful if you try to talk to your dog softly and reassuringly when he is having an "anxiety attack". Wrapping him up with a towel or blanket (or Thundershirt) helps too as dogs feel more secure when there is a constant firm feel around their bodies. These techniques require time and patience for it to become effective.

Also there are Calming Collars. These are made with herbs inside fabric to repel the aroma of calming herbs. Try diffusing Peace and Calming essential oils that contain like Lavender or other calming oils that reduce stress and anxiety. Ylang Ylang is another one.

Sometimes they work, sometimes they don't. Same goes for the Thundershirt. But it's certainly worth a try. There are also herbs you can try. These are given orally. A great website is *AldaronEssences.com*. Rescue Remedy for Pets is another herbal mix.

Veterinarians are big on handing out medications such as Acepromazine and Chlorpromazine for fearful dogs. These should **not** be given to fearful dogs. EVER! These are used during surgery as well so know what your vet uses and request an alternative.

 Acepromazine or Ace (Promace ®) and Chlorpromazine are two commonly used phenothiazine tranquilizers in veterinary clinics.

While under the effect of Ace, the animal still has a very strong fear, anxiety, avoidance or arousal response, but it does not physically display these reactions and is less able to react. The dog or cat appears calm and relaxed but mentally is lucid and still having an intense emotional reaction to its surroundings. Ace is a dissociative agent and prevents the patient from understanding his environment in a logical manner. So, the actual fear level of the animal is increased. Compounding the situation, the animal is being restrained and it makes a negative association with the entire experience.

According to veterinary behaviorist Dr. Vint Virga, DVM, ACVB, this is one of the reasons, why clinics are seeing so many animals, which have been previously given Ace, continuing to be fearful during veterinary exams. It becomes a never-ending cycle of chemical restraint and continued fear for the pet.

Ace is appropriate as a tranquilizer for the happy, jubilant, bouncy dog that has **no** anxiety, stress or fear.

Note: Ace should never be used as a tranquilizer for animals traveling due to the erratic thermoregulation effects (inability to control body temperature in cold or hot conditions).

Ace, used to sedate fearful animals, is no longer appropriate. Its use should be discontinued.

One more "don't": Whatever you do, don't lock your dog in a room or area they can escape from. Dogs have been known to get out of homes and garages, destroy crates, and break leashes and collars to escape when terrified by storms and fireworks.

CBD oil or Cannabis oil (no seeds)
Cannabis oil or CBD oil is legal in all states. This CBD/hemp oil contains less than .03 percent THC and it is considered legal under this amount in ALL STATES. I have personally been using this on my fearful dog and it has actually helped her to relax more. It doesn't take away her fears but it helps reduce the anxiety that comes with it and she rests better at night also. She isn't so restless. When purchasing CBD oil, human supplements work just as well. In fact there have

been some reports that the pet CBD oils may or may not contain any CBD oil so therefore will not work. It is hard to know without being tested. So thoroughly check out your sources and don't go by just hearsay. Pet products are also much higher in price I have seen.

 I buy organic CBD oil for humans for my dog. I found when searching for one, that the milligrams in them were/are very confusing. You have sizes that show milligrams and you have amounts that show milligrams. Ok to keep it simple, I purchased a one ounce bottle...at 300mg. Now where it gets even trickier is how much on dosing amounts. No one can really say how much. They may or may not give you dosing amounts. Most of it is guesswork. Read the label as it may tell you something like CBD extract 31 mg. per recommended dose. So I started with 5-6 drops. Then I decided to increase the amount. So I increased it to 10 drops. Now this is for a 70lb dog. I didn't feel like I was seeing any changes so I decided what the heck, I will try a dropper full. That's when I noticed that she was not so restless and was sleeping much better. This was also given over a period of 30 days. Sometimes it takes awhile to start working. It has also helped her when she gets out of the home. She's very fearful of strangers and/or strange places so this helps her to handle it slightly better. I also think once you get it built up in their system, less is needed per day. This is all about playing round with the amounts. Start low and work your way up until you see some sort of results. Give it 1-2 months. Nothing works overnight.

Other things you can try:

- Soundproofing a crate or room
- Play calming (classical or high frequency) music or white noise
- Ashwagandha daily supplement. (used for depression, anxiety etc)
- Skullcap
- Chamomile (nervine herb-used for calming)
- L-Theanine (supplement that may help calm your dog.)
- Essential oils such as Lavender, Peace & Calming or Ylang Ylang can be used for aromatherapy.

Whatever you do, don't give up on trying to calm your dog. Each dog is different so it will take you finding the right solution. I hope these things will work for you. You can even combine some of these. Good Luck!

Tip: For female dogs who exhibit signs of agitation (sometimes to the point of panic), generalized anxiety, fear of new people, other dogs or new situations, they may be deficient in estrogen as well as progesterone. Have your vet check for these things.

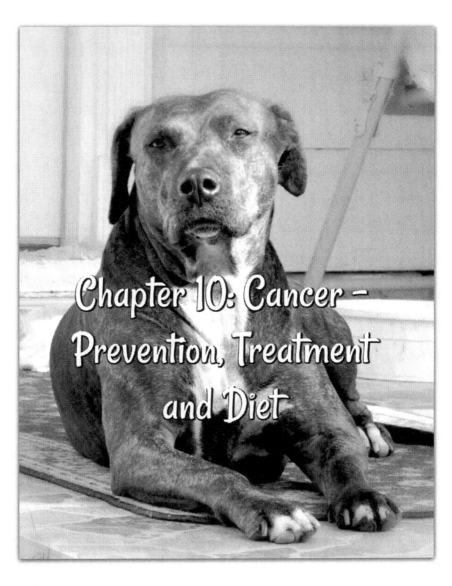

Chapter 10: Cancer - Prevention, Treatment and Diet

Chapter 10
Cancer - Prevention, Treatment and Diet

I have spent hours and hours watching many videos, webinars, symposiums and reading many articles, studying natural cancer treatments and prevention. So I am sharing with you what I have learned so that if you get that dreaded diagnosis, you will be prepared and have all the tools you need to begin the fight. All of this will be good for preventing that nasty disease as well. Being told that your dog has cancer is of course heart breaking. But don't take this as a death sentence and give up! Be proactive. Make it your mission to find out as much as you can about your dog's condition, the treatments available and what you can do yourself to help rid this horrifying disease from your dog. Some call it a fungus. I like to think of it as inflammation or infection. You may realize that there are more options than you think. Have faith and believe you can beat this. There is so much information on cancer; it will be impossible for me to even get close to the tip of the iceberg to cover all the great things you can do to fight this. But these are some of the most common things you can try at home along with or without conventional treatments.

I truly don't recommend chemo or radiation of any kind. Why? Because radiation and chemo are what comes from 2-4-D (Agent Orange) and mustard gas. Yeah, read that again. It's true. Scary thought there. I have also discovered that these treatments are the number one money making treatment in all of health care. Even though we have natural cures out there, the FDA and many other government agencies are not allowing these. Why? Because there is too much money to be made off of people and they don't care if we die anyway. Their goal is to reduce the population. Yes they are doing that too, I am not kidding and I wished I was. I learned this straight from scientist, whistle blowers and doctors. You would be shocked at what I have learned about our food, water, vaccines and medications. You can learn this too by just watching videos, seminars of Drs and many that do care about human life. So you really honestly do not want to use these chemicals to try to destroy the cancer. Even cutting into a cancer cell also allows it to spread throughout the body. So always consider this before ever considering surgery. Have your dr/vet guarantee you in writing that your dog will be cured from cancer using this type of treatment. I get worked up when I think about what's being done. It's truly horrific.

Cancer is one of the top killers in people and pets. Look at the latest numbers. The latest annual report provides the estimated numbers of new cancer cases and deaths in 2016, as well as current cancer incidence, mortality, and survival statistics and information on cancer symptoms, risk factors, early detection, and treatment. In 2016, there were approximately 1,685,210 diagnosed with cancer and 595,690 cancer deaths in the US. One out of two dogs will get cancer. That's extremely high numbers and a sad reality, unless we make changes today. Reduce the odds. Don't let your dog or you, be a statistic.

Conventional cancer treatments using chemotherapy and radiation may be effective in getting rid of or reducing cancerous tumors, but these treatments destroy the immune system as well and many times these treatments end up killing the dog or person instead of the cancer itself. Chemo and radiation also creates secondary tumors that occur within 3-5 years. It causes cancer! So make sure you decide on the correct treatment. And if you are really struggling with this decision, you can try the alternative treatments for a while and see if it is helping. Trust me; they will help in some form or fashion. If you choose conventional treatments, just know this will destroy the immune system leaving it vulnerable to fight disease and will make your dog much sicker. Even biopsies and surgeries can end up spreading the cancer further by releasing the cancer cells throughout when these cells are cut into or disturbed in any way. They need to stay contained. Many pets and people have lived many years with a tumor that has not grown or spread by using holistic modalities. When using herbs and supplements and making changes in your environment and diet, you can extend the life of your dog even if cancer is not cured. It will extend your dog's life without using harsh chemicals that will end up killing your dog sooner than you would with using natural treatments.

In the meantime you need to build the immune system the entire treatment time and keep the body's immune system strong throughout the rest of your dog's life. Do **not** get in a big hurry to make a decision on doing chemo or radiation treatments. Most all drs/vets will try to rush you into treatment immediately. This is a scare tactic used to hurry and get your money before you change your mind and find other alternative options. Cancer didn't get there overnight. It took years to grow, so there is no hurry to run out tomorrow and fix it...so to speak. Make a plan. Any plan is never set in stone and there are many options that can be done in conjunction with. So no ONE decision is the correct one. There are only a select few of aggressive growing cancers (ex: Chondrosarcoma) where immediate intervention is needed. Speak with the Oncologist on which cancer your dog has. But take a few days no matter what the diagnosis is just to get your mind right after the initial diagnosis before making a decision. And remember, there is a very high probability that conventional treatments will cause secondary cancers within 3-5 years of treatment.

It is known that certain purebred dogs also have a common inherited tendency for cancer. Cancer prone breeds include Golden Retrievers, Labradors, Bernese Mountain Dogs, Boxers, Cocker Spaniels, Rottweiler's and Beagles.

Spaying or neutering at an early age has been known to cause cancer along with commercial pet foods. All pet foods break down into at least 50% of pure sugar. Also these pet foods have been sprayed with grease or fats that become rancid and in which cause cancer as well.

Now first, let's revert back to the diet. You MUST change this if you have been feeding anything other than organic or grass-fed diets. Kibble and canned pet foods do not count. You cannot feed these if your dog has cancer. You MUST clean the entire body of toxins inside and out. There is a Ketogenic diet that is coming out for pets. It consists of quality meat proteins and healthy fats. In place of carbs, you replace with healthy fats. Healthy fats include Olive oil, Ghee or grass-fed butter, Coconut oil, eggs, organic nuts (small amounts), fish oil, avocado's (no pits) and pasture-fed and/or organic meats. It also consists of adding in organic green leafy veggies in raw pureed form or finely chopped.

Ketogenic Diets (all organic/pasture-fed)
If your dog has cancer or any type of illness or disease for example seizures, auto-immune; this may be a good diet for your dog. This is close to the raw diet but you add in more healthy fats, reduce the meat and a small amount of carbs (leafy greens). This is a diet for your dog with cancer. This is not to use forever. Any diet should always have variety so you will be changing this diet often (4 months) depending on dogs' condition. Fasting is more of the preferred recommendation. There are different levels or adjustments in this diet depending on weight and the reduction of the tumor(s). Once a person and or animal acquires cancer, the odds of cancer coming back are always there. So

you will need to continue your supplements and a monitored diet (not necessarily the Ketogenic diet) throughout to keep it from ever returning.

If feeding kibble, canned, packaged commercial foods, change to an organic homemade raw immediately following this books recommendations.

If your dog has gone through or going through Chemo, you may want to purchase raw meats that has been sterilized or better known as **High Pressure Pasteurization**. Without strict measuring of this diet or using calorie restriction, you can cause high blood glucose levels.

In a Ketogenic diet, you will feed less meat than on a normal raw diet and add in more healthy fats and a few green leafy veggies. This is the basics of the diet. I highly recommend if you want to do the Ketogenic diet, to contact Ketopet Sanctuary or purchase the Truth About Pet Cancer series for the break down on how to measure each food item in detail. There is a lot of math to it for every dog's weight. To give you an idea, it goes something like this. You will feed approximately15 calories per the weight of your dog. So a 50 lb dog x 15 calories = 750 calories per day. If you have an obese dog, you will use 10 calories per weight. For an already raw fed dog or to get into ketosis the fastest, you will use a 4:1 ratio (90% healthy fats, 9% protein and 1% carbs). A maintenance type Ketogenic diet would be 0.5:1 ratio (53% healthy fats, 46% protein and 1% carbs). (4 calories per gram of protein, 4 calories per gram of carbs, 9 calories per gram of fats). Weigh your dog weekly. **I do not recommend this diet without having all the details on percentages. Work closely with a knowledgeable party such as Ketopet Sanctuary before trying this on your own.**

Healthy Fats *(Start low and work up to higher amounts if not already in the diet)*
Organic Coconut oil or powder
MCT oil or powder
Fish oils (small fish)
Avocado oil (avocado pits are toxic, not the avocado itself)
Organic Extra Virgin Olive oil
Organic Raw nuts (excluding Macadamia nuts) (small amounts)

Organic Ghee (butter) or grass-fed unsalted butter
Organic Hempseed oil
Beef Tallow
Duck Fat

Meats (pasture-fed and/or organic only)
Rabbit
Goat
Beef
Poultry
Wild Game of any kind

Fish:
Sardines
Anchovies
Salmon

Organic Veggies (Finely chopped or pureed-raw only)
Cauliflower
Cabbage
Celery
Brussels Sprouts
Asparagus
Broccoli
Kale
Spinach
Zucchini
Green Beans
Collard Greens

Other:
Organic Homemade Bone Broth
Raw milk
Fermented yogurt or kefir
Homemade kefir with no sugar (using kefir grains)
Organic or pasture-fed eggs
Raw organic cheese
Apple Cider Vinegar
Bully sticks for treats

Do not feed:
Grains of any kind
Flour/breads
Honey
Molasses
Potatoes of any kind
All Fruit
Squash
Carrots
Beets
Corn
Peas
Peppers
Pumpkin
Turnips

If you need to give medications or pills in any form, try putting into ghee or grass fed butter or raw cheese or directly into the meal itself.

(Ketoacidosis and Ketosis not the same) Ketoacidosis refers to diabetic ketoacidosis (DKA) and is a complication of type 1 diabetes. It is high levels of ketones and blood sugar. This combination makes your blood too acidic, which can change the normal functioning of internal organs like your liver and kidneys. This is not the same as **Ketosis**. Your dog can be in ketosis if he/she is on a low-carb diet or fasting. Ketones are a chemical your body produces when it burns stored fat for energy instead of relying on sugars. Also a Ketogenic diet has been known to reduce seizures in pets.

So to check your dog to see if he is in Nutritional Ketosis, have your vet check the glucose and ketones. Although these would be better checked often. They do make an at-home kit to check for this called Precision Xtra Blood Glucose & Ketone Monitoring System for around $40-$50. It's made for humans but you can still use it for your dog. It's in with the diabetic products in pharmacies. You will need to prick for a tad of blood so you will need lancets. Don't forget the strips that go with it. You can prick them in areas such as elbows or paw pad above the foot. Also an ear is a good place or inside the side of the mouth in the flap of the jowls. You can do this a couple times a week to check it in the beginning prior to meal time. As you level off, you can check it like once a week. There are videos on YouTube to watch on how to do this.

If your dog is in nutritional ketosis, the blood ketones will range from 0.3m/mol to 0.8m/mol and blood glucose between 60mg/dL - 80mg/dL. These are rough estimates but ballpark figures to work within and what you will be working off of on adjusting the diet.

Ketopet Sanctuary is the people that have developed this diet for dogs with cancer and have perfected it. They also use Hyperbaric Oxygen Chambers as well.

If your dog has been diagnosed with cancer, an intermittent or pulsed fasting can/should be done. You will feed meals within 6-8 hours *(pulsed)*, and then fast till the next day at the same time each day. This helps the body to go into ketosis. You can also fast your dog several times a week. Calorie restriction is important.

As for cooking the food, dogs **cannot digest cooked animal fats** like humans can. This could also increase the risk of pancreatitis. Keeping fats and proteins raw is feeding a species appreciate diet as they would in the wild. Some people worry about feeding raw diets with dogs with cancer. This would be when you should seek the advice of a holistic vet or Oncologist that knows about raw diets or the Ketopet Sanctuary for more information. But overall, raw diets are usually always acceptable.

Once you have a diagnosis of cancer or you want to prevent cancer, follow this protocol. Now I want you to know that it is very important to add supplements in at this time. You must do this and not just one supplement will cure your dog. Not the perfect diet will cure him/her either. It is a combination of things. They all need to come together to cure your dog. This will take hard work, time, patience and a few extra dollars in your pocket. Supplements are not cheap (neither is chemo) and you will be using many different ones. But it's cheaper than conventional treatments. So get prepared to do everything different if you haven't had your dog on a homemade diet already. This will be a fast learning course and this book will tell you how. Despite articles on the internet saying cancer is down, this is simply not true. How many family or friends that you know have passed away or been diagnosed with this horrible disease? One in three people die or get cancer. The numbers are up on our family pets as well. Every day you hear about a pet being put down or dying from cancer. It's time to be proactive.

Why are we getting cancer at alarming rates? Many reasons and it all revolves around our own government. In the USA, we have the FDA. The very people that are supposed to be protecting us are the ones harming us. They are in cahoots with Big Pharma and Monsanto. We have Monsanto and DuPont and others that are adding chemicals to everything, genetically modifying our foods and using pest resistant pesticides that are getting into our soils and our foods and slowly poisoning us. It's been mentioned time and time again about the FDA and what they seem to **not** be doing. Don't trust our government to protect us. It is those very people that are destroying us. Bill Gates (creator of Windows for computers) is pushing vaccines to reduce the population. Hitler used Fluoride to dumb down the human population and make them docile and obey orders (and it's still happening to us today). Watch out for those flu vaccines and alike. You think it stops there? Not even close. So learn, be aware and always research before giving anything to your pet. You have options. Find the one best for you.

Water *(filtered fluoride and chlorine free including pesticides, chemicals etc)*

Many chemicals are in our tap waters. Over 60,000 to be exact. Chemicals and preservatives are also in our medications, vaccines, foods, and the air we breathe. We put it on our lawns and wash our clothes in chemicals. It's overwhelming. Our bodies just cannot protect us from getting sick or diseased from so many chemicals overloading our immune systems. It just doesn't have a chance to fight so many. So we must reduce these toxins as much as possible. Start with the food and water. You can test your water for chemicals and pesticides by doing a simple water test. But ALWAYS buy one that also filters out fluoride and chlorine. I find so many people with water filters that have not even considered the fluoride. Fluoride is a drug. This stuff is toxic. These both are now considered a neurotoxin. Don't take this lightly. Remove all of these chemicals from your home.

Make huge changes here. It's critical for everyone. Water is just as important as the food.

Buy organic and/or pasture-fed eggs. You will see egg cartons saying cage free. What does that mean? NOTHING! It means nothing! A chicken is out of a cage but packed into a barn and the chickens still can't flap their wings. They are eating grains like GMO corn. When you eat that chicken or egg, you are getting what they eat going into your body as well. So buy organic/pasture-fed eggs or chickens. Even if it isn't organic, pasture-fed is so much better than cage free. Also when it says in the stores the chicken says "hormone and antibiotic free"; not true! Ask any holistic integrative doctor or vet.
I know this book is for dogs but everything in it also applies to humans. We must be the change. We must protect our bodies and heal them using what God gave us; the plants from our earth. In 2022 they are coming out with a stronger and more deadly pesticide than Round Up. The main ingredient of Round up is Glyphosate. It's on our wheat and most every food out there unless organic. Then you question how much is getting sprayed in the air and falling onto our organic foods. But organic is your best bet no matter what.

When you throw all of these things into one pot (your body and your pets), you have a recipe for disaster. Cancer is inevitable unless you have a strong healthy immune system. You can choose to stick your head in the sand or better yet, make some changes to help prevent and protect your loved ones and you. I had someone ask for help recently. Their dog has cancer. I explained in a very respectful simple way that she really needed her dog off kibble and on a homemade diet and was going to have to add in supplements and makes some big changes to save her dog. I never heard from her again. This is what makes me sad. It's hard for me to understand that type of person. I would give my left arm for my dogs and do whatever I could to save them if I thought there was even a remote chance.

So to start, you must change the diet, provide filtered (multi-stage filter) fluoride/chlorine free water along with an Ionizer /Alkalizer, stop **all** vaccines and medications (if possible), and remove chemicals and toxins from your home. You should see the inactive ingredients in medications. They are horrible. Food dyes, propylene glycol and so

many other horrible ingredients. For water filters, a reverse osmosis works very well and add on a fluoride filter as well. You cannot avoid everything but you can make a huge dent in avoiding many by doing a few things differently. And in by doing this, you can help reduce you and your dog's chances of getting cancer or feeding the cancer.
There are 85,000+ chemicals being used today in this world. There are new ones being invented every day. So start with cleaning out your home, your lawn, your foods and your water. Throw away the foods that are GMO or processed foods. Things such as boxed foods as well as canned. BPA is in the lining of cans. You want clean foods in your house. Rid your home of chemicals. Store bought bleach, dryer sheets, laundry detergents, sprays such as air fresheners, furniture polish, Windex etc. Don't worry, there are alternatives.

Stock up on vinegar and baking soda and a few nice smelling safe essential oils to use around all pets. Buy organic non-chemical laundry detergents. I like the brand called FIT laundry detergent. Use dryer balls in dryer. (It's better for your dryer anyway) but if you insist on using dryer sheets, Meyers makes some that I know are safe. Clean your carpets using vinegar and water. Mop using the same or water only. You can make your own home-made window cleaner. I make my own using 1 part rubbing alcohol, 2 parts water, and a few drops of a nice smelling essential oil. You can even make stain removers for clothes. I use 1 part Dawn dishwashing liquid, 2 parts water, and 1 part Hydrogen Peroxide. The internet is full of natural ways of doing things. Again learn ingredients. If you aren't sure, go to sites like EWG.org and do a search. It will give you an idea. The best thing you can do for your dog and family is learning to read labels. Pay special attention to supplements and medications with the INACTIVE ingredients. That's where you find a lot of the toxic chemicals and/or fillers. I call these JUNK ingredients.

Get your dog off of commercial pet foods of all kinds period. Yes, this is a must! It is at the top of the list of what is causing cancer as well as many other diseases in our pets today. With so many mycotoxins and preservatives, it's inevitable. This applies to human foods as well. (Buy organic, organic, organic or pasture-fed).
The best diet you can feed your pets is a homemade raw diet. In

cancer when you feed a Ketogenic diet, the diet needs to be raw to help prevent Pancreatitis. Veggies can be given in raw juiced/pureed or in a steamed form. Raw form is always better. Steamed is second best. You will need to add in some supplements. Many supplements are sourced from China much of the time so it's best to try to find vitamins in a natural form. Whole foods like an organic greens powder and/or organic veggies and fruits. If you provide fresh organic raw veggies and fruits to your dog, make sure you puree/juice them or finely chop them up. Dogs cannot digest chunks of veggies and some fruits so they need help to get the nutrients needed from them. Fruits are softer and do digest easier so eating small chunks is fine but you can puree these as well. Keep fruits at a bare minimum. Yes fruits contain natural sugars but are fine in small amounts on occasion. Fruits with lower sugar content are best. As for cooking your dog's food, it removes a lot of nutrients that may be needed and it is harder to digest than raw. You will need to add in supplements no matter how the food is prepared. I have created a list in this book and on my website for supplements needed to be added to any and all diets. I am always updating them when I find even better things. Remove dairy (with exception of raw or fermented), sugar, carbs (potatoes) of all kinds (no grains of any kind).

Remember, cancer cannot survive in an oxygen enriched blood supply so therefore adding oxygenated supplements and/or foods to the diet are important. Also look into Hyperbaric Oxygen Chambers. Hyperbaric Oxygen Chambers are really a great tool. They can be expensive ($135 per session) but it will get oxygen into the blood fast and start killing cancer. You may get grief from your vet or therapist that you work with using natural sources but stick to your guns, provide them with only information that they REALLY need. But do the hyperbaric chamber if you can add it in. I feel this is a critical therapy in beating cancer. Also invest in a good HEPA air purifier for your home. Buy several and place in main rooms and where your dog and you sleep.

Get rid of the plastic food and water bowls. Make sure you use glass, high quality ceramic or stainless. I use dinner plates for my dog's raw diet every day.
Dogs are extremely sensitive to EMF (Electro Magnetic Frequency) and Radio frequency waves. That would include cell phones, Wi-Fi,

and Smart TV's. Anything you can plug in. That includes your electric toothbrush, computer and more. Unplug these things when not in use and turn off your Wi-Fi as well. These make people sick and even our pets as they are much more sensitive than us humans. Start turning these things off when not in use and see if you notice any difference. Give it some time to see any changes. It may take awhile but you will reduce exposure to all of these radiation waves.

Do not use fertilizers or weed killers on your lawn. They do however make all organic natural ingredients completely safe for pets and kids. Some may work, some may not. Use Diatomaceous earth (food grade only) for pest control. For insect control, you can try using Borax (laundry) but don't let the dogs eat it. It isn't to be ingested. They also make products that are all natural for this or mix your own. You can find many recipes on the internet. Remember, learn to read all ingredients. If you don't know them, Google it. Research before you buy or use. I have a huge list of these junk ingredients that are in medications and foods on my websites as well.

After walking dogs in public places, wash off the paws by sticking them in a bowl of water with some raw unfiltered apple cider vinegar or Povidone iodine and water (dark tea colored) added in for a few minutes, then wipe/pat dry.

Do **not** use any topical flea and tick medications. These are deadly and full of toxic chemicals. Use all natural products. Find one that works best for you. A lot of these contain essential oils. Stay away from some of the oils no matter who sells it.

Listed below in the graph are some essential oils to **avoid** using on your pets skin or ingesting. I would avoid diffusing these as well unless specifically directed by a holistic vet.

If you have cats or small children, you may want to avoid most essential oils or do extensive research.

Anise	Boldo
Birsch	Calamus

Bitter Almond	Camphor
Cassia	Chenopodium
Clove Leaf and Bud	Crested Lavender
Garlic	Tea Tree Oil
Goosefoot	Horseradish
Hyssop (use decumbens variety only)	Juniper (use j. berry only)
Mugwort	Mustard
Oregano	Pennyroyal (toxic to kidneys)
Red or White Thyme	Rue
Santalina	Sassafras
Savory	Tansy
Terebinth	Thuja
Wintergreen	Wormwood
Yarrow	

Work with a holistic vet before using these essential oils that I have listed but avoid them in OTC products for pets unless your vet gives you the ok. Essential oils should be diluted with a carrier oil or alike such as coconut oil etc.

You may need to experiment with different natural flea and tick products but they do exist and work well when used correctly. Add some scented herbs and plants around your yard that repels. Like peppermint, lavender, lemongrass, eucalyptus etc.

And for goodness sake's, DO NOT SMOKE around your pets! Stay at least 50 feet from your pets when smoking. Go outside to smoke but do not allow them out with you.

Vaccines!
DO NOT vaccinate your pet **at all** if he/she has been diagnosed with cancer. That includes the Rabies vaccine. Get a waiver. Every time you turn around, a new vaccine has been invented/created for some sort of new disease. It's totally nuts. Vaccines contain mercury and aluminum and other toxins including preservatives and bacteria.

These are the very things that cause cancer. Do not buy into what your vet may tell you. The flu vaccines for people and for pets are nothing more than a moneymaker for the people that created them. I even read where they are adding something into the human flu vaccines to reduce sperm counts in men so to reduce population. I know, it's crazy. We just don't know do we?

If you do everything listed here, you will not have to be concerned about the flu. Give your dog the 3-year rabies vaccine every 3 years if they do **not** have cancer. Your vet must be on the same page as this. Yes they make a 3-year vaccine. Request it before ever going in to see your vet.

If they do not offer it, find a new vet. Their mission isn't about helping your dog. Puppies should have their vaccines to help protect them getting through their younger years. Some vaccines may be better off avoided. If you have a concern about the protection they may have against certain diseases, try titers. Have your vet sign up with Vaccicheck or check out Dr Robb at ProtectThePets.com. Titer test for antibodies. Over all, a vaccine is a cancer causing injection and to repeat these year after year, can become fatal.

For small dogs less than 12 lbs, ask for half the vaccine. You can request this with all vaccines except for Rabies. Yep, a 12 lb dog gets the same dose as a 100 lb dog. The law requires the FULL dose of the Rabies vaccine. Ugh! The risks involved with that are extremely high. Vaccines also can cause diseases and joint issues. Even aggression in some dogs.

Before, during, and after a Rabies vaccine, you can use nosode pellets to help curb any reactions or side effects to it. Using Lyssin (preferably 200c) for Rabies vaccines. Thuja is used for the other vaccines. But it doesn't reduce the toxins taken in. The vaccine is still doing its damage to the system. Ask for the Thimerosal-Free Rabies vaccine (Merial IMRAB TF). Again if your dog has cancer, get a waiver. Vaccines are NOT to be given to sick pets at all. The manufacture prints that on the labels and/or warning labels and have your vet read this so he can get your message that you know what you are saying. So you have every right and a good argument for not giving a Rabies

vaccine to a dog with cancer. Any vet that forces this upon you, walk out that door and find a holistic vet or one that's not pushy.
Also know that spaying/neutering your dog too early can cause problems with the endocrine system and also create cancers as well. It is recommended to wait till at least 18 months to spay/neuter.
Any time you put medications and vaccines into the body, you are adding toxins that can grow cancer cells. Avoid all as much as possible. If your dog has cancer, limit the use of all medications if at all humanly possible. There are herbs to help with certain issues. Much safer than medications of any kind.

I have to tell you a story. I spoke with someone one day helping them with their dog that has joint issues. In our conversation she bragged about how wonderful her vet was. She went on and on and on about her wonderful vet. Well, then we got into this discussion about vaccines. She said to me, "My vet says it is **"by law"** that dogs get the Bordetella vaccine every time they stay at their clinic". Wait what? I was in shock. This woman was also a nurse. She had no idea. Her dog gets a Bordetella vaccine like every month. I told her that was incorrect and that the Bordetella vaccine does not work. And it should NEVER be required. This is the type of vet you want to **avoid at all costs.** You are paying the bill. It is YOUR RIGHT and your decision on vaccines. If they cannot agree to your way, find a vet that will. Remember your vet works for you. I can't stress this enough!

Kennel cough (Bordetella) is equivalent to the human cold. A vaccine isn't going to fix or avoid this. Again this is for moneymaking purposes. Kennel cough is however contagious so make sure you keep pets separated until it passes. Give your dog Echinacea, Astragalus and Mullein until well.

The FDA is well aware of cures and all natural treatments for cancer but it is not allowed to be marketed or advertised. In fact Big Pharma (and others) has a say so in that. Doctors that have used and are treating patients with cancer using all-natural treatments and that have actually cured cancer are being criticized and harassed by our own government. Some have been thought to have been murdered. Some have been shot, homes and businesses raided, multiple Supreme Court hearings trying to put these life saving Drs in prison, and for what, saving a life. Wrap your brain around that one for a minute. Mind blowing. In Mexico it is legal for these natural treatments and there are several cancer centers in Tijuana. So we must take this into our own hands to cure ourselves and our pets here in the U.S.A. since we are not given any choices.

There is also a doctor that's here in Texas that uses anti-neoplastons to cure cancers and he has succeeded many times. It's a long story but, he has been in front of the supreme court like 6-7 times. Even the mainstream media has ridiculed him and called him a quack. It is the FDA and the Texas State Medical Board that's harassing him. He even has an FDA approval to use this patented concoction but yet, they still want him behind bars so they can steal his work. He invented this cure and patented it. He was fined $60,000 during the last court hearing but kept his license that they were trying to revoke. This man is brilliant. The point is, the government is trying to stop cancer cures. There is too much money to be made on sick people. This is our government. So we MUST learn what we can ourselves and do what we have to do to cure ourselves and our pets. Don't be afraid. What do you have to lose?

I keep talking about this because I want people to know, this is really happening and how critical it is to know what you are dealing with and up against. We have been brainwashed to think chemotherapy is the cure and it's just not. I am trying to reiterate that into your brain that this is wrong. Think about how they could care less for our pets?

Supplements
Make sure you add in supplements listed below into the diet to help prevent and treat cancer and other diseases. These have been known to prevent and/or destroy cancer cells. Use organic any chance you can. I added some recommended supplements to help build the immune system since cancer feeds off of weakened immune systems. You do not need to run out and buy them all; find the ones that you feel will work best for you to start. Don't be overwhelmed. It will all fall into place as you go. I do however recommend several important ones. The Apricot kernels/B-17 capsules, Humic/Fulvic acid, Probiotics and Digestive Enzymes and a good mix of anti-inflammatory herbs. Also Cell Stop appears to build the immune system and offers

herbs for taking out those cancer cells. Read on all the other supplements to see what you may want to add. A good combination of these will help battle cancer as well as help prevent it. Preventative doses will be lower than doses for diagnosed cancers.

These supplements will help to detox the body, help kill cancer cells and build the immune system. If you do happen to cure your dog's cancer, your dog will still have to remain on the same regimen but with lower doses. You may be able to eliminate some of these supplements but you will have to remain on the ones I listed above for the life of the dog. Also the same diet as well. This is life changing. If your dog doesn't have cancer, change the diet right away, homemade organic or grass-fed. Start now. Prevention has always been the best medicine. Before you can prevent the disease you have to understand it.

Let's get down to the details on supplements now shall we.

CBD for Dogs (cannabinoids)

Numerous studies have found cannabinoids and particularly CBD to have anti-tumor effects and anti-inflammatory properties. Additionally, CBD has been shown to regulate and stimulate appetite, modulate pain and improve the overall vitality and health of animals.

There is a lot of hype about Cannabis oils (CBD) going on and let's talk about them. This is my opinion but I am still doing my research on it. It is a good addition to the dog's diet. All 50 states allow the purchase of CBD oils that do not contain THC or less than.03 percent. While this may or may not fight certain cancers, it can help relieve pain, reduce stress and help reduce tumors in certain cases. It can help many ailments and I will always recommend this as an addition to using other supplements. I wouldn't use it alone for treating cancer unless you have a medical card allowed by states where it is legal. Only the CBD oil that is over the legal limit with THC that will have the profound effects on killing cancer.

Remember, you can't cure cancer using ONE ingredient. It takes an army to knock down this enemy. The medicinal CBD oils that contain over .03 percent are illegal in most states although this is changing every day. THC actually kills the cancer more so. Suppositories do not cause any high effects. CBD oils do not cause a toxic effect. It is used for medicinal purposes only. Make sure your CBD is from the leaves, buds, and **flowers.** Not from seeds. And also it is processed through what is called solvent extraction. Not pressing and usually done with seeds.

Organic Greens Powder (Blend)
Organic Greens Powder or juicing (pureed or finely chopped raw veggies). Organic greens and veggies are full of natural vitamins and minerals and is the key to healing the digestive system. When your digestive system isn't functioning properly, then you are open to disease and illness. Absorbing raw nutrients from the greens (powdered or juiced) provides your much-needed body and your dogs, a path to building a strong immune system. This is important for recovery and prevention. These can also help heal a leaky gut. Leaky gut can cause cancer as well. Leaky gut is determined by small holes in the lining of the intestines therefore leaking out foods, toxins etc into the bloodstream causing cancer and many other illnesses and disease.

What causes Leaky Gut? Well it's from a poor diet and vitamin deficiencies to keep it simple. Using greens high in chlorophyll helps to rebuild the lining. Also using probiotics, digestive enzymes and Slippery Elm will help. Feeding organic is best. You need to keep all those chemicals and pesticides out of the body. Many of our foods are layered with Glyphosate. Regular foods are GMO foods. Both will cause severe intestinal issues including Irritable Bowel Disease (IBD), allergies, bad behaviors and much more.

Dosing for greens powder:
Small dogs: 1/4-1/2 teaspoon
Medium/Large dogs: 1/2-1 teaspoon
Giant dogs: 1-1 1/2 teaspoons

Also it is known that iodine in the body helps to conquer cancer cells, so provide a small amount of Kelp or some type of sea-iodine if not giving the greens powder blend.

Digestive Enzymes and Probiotics (Recommended)
Builds a strong digestive tract, weeds out the bad bacteria and adds in the good. Great for building a strong well functioning digestive tract.

This is important in every cancer patient's diet. Double dosing recommended.

Humic/Fulvic Acid (Recommended)
It can be very beneficial to take a double or even a triple dose, depending on body size and severity of your health issues. This contains over 90 natural occurring plant derived minerals, trace elements, vitamins, and amino acids in an unaltered ionic solution. It increases oxygen absorption into the blood. Remember, oxygen enriched blood kills cancer cells.

In a perfect world we would all consume nutrient rich fruits and vegetables and there would be no need to supplement our diets with Fulvic; it would be readily available in our food supply.

Unfortunately, our current farming practices use chemicals and pesticides that kill the microorganisms that create Fulvic, and because of this, Fulvic minerals are severely lacking in today's fruits and vegetables. Even our farm animals, which are now consuming Fulvic deficient greens, are mineral deficient themselves.

Do not give Humic/Fulvic acid with medications or juice. Allow 2 hours in-between for best absorption..

Dosage:
Small dogs: 1 teaspoon
Medium dogs: 2 teaspoons
Large dogs: 1 TBSP
Or follow label on human dosing.

Apricot Seed/Kernels (B-17 / Amygdalin/Laetrile) (Raw and Bitter) *(works well on Breast, Lung, Colon and Prostate and many other cancers)*

This is an important food to take for killing and preventing cancer. You want ORGANIC RAW BITTER SEEDS. The more bitter the better. Seeds that are not bitter do not work for cancer. Each kernel contains 20mg of B-17/Laetrile/Amygdalin.

For actual seeds/kernels dosage for treating cancer:

Approximate Dosage:
Preventive doses:
2-4 seeds up to 50lb dogs or (100-200mg in capsules)
5-8 seeds for 50-100 lb dogs (200-300mg in capsules)
10-12 seeds for over 100lbs (300-400mg capsules)

For cancer treatment, see dosage below.

If nausea or loss of appetite occurs, just reduce the amount you are using daily.
You can grind these up or buy the already ground up organic ones.

Cancer Treatment Dosing:
For actual seeds/kernels to treat aggressive or late stage cancer in dogs:
5-10 seeds/kernels (100-200mg Amygdalin/B-17) up to 50lbs
10-15 seeds/kernels (200-300mg Amygdalin/B-17) for 50-100 lbs
15-20 seeds/kernels (300-400mg Amygdalin/B-17) over 100 lbs
*You will **not** give this for first dose. You need to work up to this amount over a period of a few weeks.*

You can give up to 600mg (30 kernels) of Amygdalin/B-17 safely in med/large dogs. Give less (400mg) for smaller dogs. To cut down on that many kernels, you can use both the kernels and capsules. The kernels contain B-15 also which is needed to help absorb the B-17. B-17 is the killing agent. They do also make a capsule of B-15 you can take as well. There are several ways to do this. What I would do is either buy the capsules of both the B-17 and B-15 or I would buy the raw bitter organic ground up kernels already and put into capsules for myself. Then buy the straight B-17 capsules to take as well. For my dogs, I would try putting the ground up kernels in food (which may have a bitter taste) and empty the B-17 capsules into the food. So I would buy the same things but put the ground up kernels in capsules for myself and empty the purchased B-17 capsules for them into food. It would go something like this:

Half the amount of Kernels
B-17 capsules
Or

B-15 capsules
B-17 capsules

Vitamin C helps to absorb B-17. So does zinc (be careful with zinc in higher amounts) and B-15. B-15 is also in the kernels. No need to add this in if you use the kernels. Capsules come in 100mg and 500mg sizes. I would recommend the 100mg to start. If there is cancer and it's at a critical timed treatment stage, I would use both capsules and kernels. There are other types of capsules that are the whole kernels. So doing the math is critical. Remember you can use up to 600mg safely. What I mean by "safely" is the side effects. They include headache and nausea. Well we don't know if dogs get headaches do we, so look for loss of appetite or maybe vomiting or diarrhea. When you get to a point that you don't think this is working or your dog is declining fast, you may want to try the higher amount. If there are any signs of vomiting, loss of appetite or diarrhea, just back off on the dose. The same thing happens when taking a higher amount of vitamin C. It isn't going to kill you but you may not feel so well or may have GI upset. You have reached your limit at that point so back off some but continue with treatment.

 For example, if my dog had cancer and was at its late stages or the dog was starting to show signs of declining health, I would increase the amount of kernels by two a day...every couple of days up to the point of loss of appetite, diarrhea or vomiting. I would probably push the limits on supplements. I wouldn't feel I had anything to lose at that point. But you use your own judgment and don't be afraid to take an extra step if your dog is at a critical stage.

*Note on the fear of eating foods that contain cyanide: Amygdalin contains four substances. Two are glucose; one is benzaldyhide, and one is cyanide. Yes, cyanide and benzaldyhide are poisons **if** they are released or freed as pure molecules and not bound within other molecular formations. Many foods containing cyanide are safe because the cyanide remains bound and locked as part of another molecule and therefore cannot cause any harm. There are 1400 foods we eat every day that contain Laetrile (Cyanide). Laetrile/Amygdalin/B-17 is in our foods but the amounts are much lower and because of nutrient*

deficient soils, the amounts are even lower. Apricot kernels have the highest amount therefore the best option for fighting cancer.
If your dog has been diagnosed with cancer in its early stages, I would work somewhere in-between the preventative dosage and the late stage dosage. Also if the tumor is in a life threatening area such as brain, near the brain or an organ, I would use the higher doses but start low and work your way up. Don't overwhelm the body too fast. Let it adjust to what's going in. This is important.

Curcumin (found in turmeric)
The herbal compound Curcumin has a mechanism of action as a natural COX-2 inhibitor (COX-2 is an inflammatory enzyme). Inhibitors of this type have shown to have the capability to help relieve common everyday inflammations triggered by a host of lifestyle factors.

- It helps to reduce the risk of ulcers due to stress and drugs by increasing the mucous protective lining of the stomach.
- It can also help to reduce elevated blood cholesterol levels and has a protective effect on the liver.
- Is a natural antiseptic and antibacterial agent, useful in disinfecting cuts and burns.
- May prevent metastases from occurring in many different forms of cancer.
- Works as an anti-inflammatory agent for arthritis and rheumatoid arthritis by lowering histamine levels.
- Is a natural painkiller and cox-2 inhibitor. In many instances, works as well as anti-inflammatory drugs but without the side effects and potential risks associated with NSAIDs.
- Used in treating depression. (Yes, dogs can suffer with depression)
- Has been shown to stop the growth of new blood vessels in tumors.
- Speeds up wound healing and assists in remodeling of damaged skin and other inflammatory skin conditions.
- By enhancing liver function, helps to cleanse the blood of toxins and impurities.

- Helps to regulate intestinal flora if taken during and after a course of antibiotics by dogs suffering with Candida (yeast infection).

Buy organic and do not buy any types (including organic) that comes from China or India. This includes Ginger, Turmeric and Garlic spices.

Ginger
Ginger, a cousin spice of super anti-cancer substance turmeric, is known for its ability to shrink tumors. Astoundingly, it is even more effective than many cancer drugs, which have been shown to be completely ineffective and actually accelerate the death of cancer patients. Commonly consumed across the world in small doses among food and beverage products, the medicinal properties of ginger far surpass even advanced pharmaceutical inventions. Also is a good treatment for chemo side effects like nausea.

Salvestrol Platinum
Salvestrols may not be effective for cats because they do not produce the CYP1B1 enzyme the same way as humans, but the results for dogs may actually be greater. Use one Salvestrol Platinum capsule (1,000 points) for up to two meals per day for every 40 pounds of dog's weight. For smaller dogs, empty the contents of the capsule proportionally by the pet's weight into your dog's food. If the dog doesn't respond after two weeks, gradually increase the dosage up to two capsules per meal for every 40 pounds. Salvestrol capsules should be taken with meals.

Avoid using apricot kernels, CBD oil of any kind, and Resveratrol while using Salvestrol. Gingko biloba, Ginseng and St. John's Wort can interfere as well. Artificial sweeteners, including Stevia, can interfere with the absorption of Salvestrols also.

*NOTE: Why Resveratrol is not listed here in this Chapter for cancer. The reason is, I have found that **higher** amounts of Resveratrol may actually increase the growth of cancer. I wouldn't want to chance where that fine line is, so I switched to recommending Salvestrols which appears to be better and stronger and can be used safely in* *higher amounts without causing cancer growth. But you will find Resveratrol mentioned often for cancer treatment.*

Not many people know about Salvestrols. I found thousands and thousands of comments from people (over 2600 pages to be exact) using this for cancer on how well Salvestrol Platinum worked and even for their dogs.

Salvestrols in North America **do not** contain grape extracts in which grape SKINS/MEAT are toxic to dogs. (Grape **seeds** are **not** toxic.) Salvestrols in North America do not contain grape extracts nor are the compounds extracted from grape products.

Note: Many of your Resveratrol products contain grapes.

Specific enhancers to Salvestrols are Niacin (Vitamin B-3), **methyl**cobalamin (vitamin B-12), magnesium, and selenium so you can add these into the diet in small amounts.

Cats Claw-Cancer (particularly urinary tract cancer)
Works on Allergies (environmental), Alzheimer's (canine), Asthma, Arthritis, Osteoarthritis as well as Rheumatoid Arthritis. Can also have effect on the blood, eyes, lungs, heart and nerves.

Also works against:
- Chronic fatigue
- Digestive System disorders – i.e.
- Colitis
- Gastritis
- Stomach ulcers
- Leaky Gut Syndrome
- Cancer (particularly urinary tract cancer)
- Cleansing of the kidneys
- Parasites
- Viral infections
- Wound Healing

If your dog has low blood pressure, Cat's Claw may lower blood pressure even more. If your dog has leukemia, do not give Cat's Claw.

Cat's Claw may help create support for the intestinal and immune systems of the body, and may also create intestinal support with its ability to cleanse the entire intestinal tract. This cleansing helps create support for people and pets experiencing different stomach and bowel disorders, including: Colitis, Crohn's disease, Irritable Bowel Syndrome, and Leaky Gut Syndrome.

Organic Sulfur
Organic sulphur has been known to turn malignant tumors into benign tumors. Add this to the daily regimen. Remember, the difference between true "organic sulfur" and inferior MSM (especially with added chemicals) is so important it could mean the difference between life and death when using this protocol!!!
Air is 21% oxygen. Water is 89% oxygen. The oxygen from air gets to the lungs, heart and muscles. However, it is the oxygen from water that needs to get inside the cells both to make the cells healthy, to give them energy and to kill microbes inside the cells.
True organic sulfur is what grabs the oxygen from the water and transports the oxygen inside the cells. This produces a surge of oxygen into the cancer cells.

True organic sulfur is important in the treatment of cancer, brain disorders and many other health conditions! Every part of the human body (including the brain) is made of cells. Getting sulfur and oxygen inside these cells is critical for all aspects of health!
So remember to drink FILTERED water with organic sulfur. For dogs, I would recommend adding to wet foods that contain a lot of moisture like raw diets do.
Wait at least 30 minutes after using Organic Sulfur before adding other supplements into the daily regimen. Organic sulfur only stays in the body for 12 hours so this will need to be given twice a day at least. This may need to be given in fairly larger amounts than what any label tells you or any normal dose. There is nothing normal about having cancer so dosages in most products will need to be much

higher. Always watch for the poop change. If diarrhea or loose stools, simply reduce amount a little until you get to a point of no diarrhea or loose stools. If for some reason your dog vomits, you may have to reduce or eliminate this from the diet. Some dogs have sensitive tummies with using this supplement.

Flaxseed oil (keep amounts low)
Flaxseed oil mixed with small curd organic cottage cheese is used in the Budwig Diet for humans, has also been reported to be effective against dog cancers. I do NOT recommend this diet alone. For one, flaxseed oil or powders usually aren't organic. If you do find some that are organic, the ALA is hard for a dog to break down into Omega-3 fatty acids. Fish oils don't need to be broken down and are easily absorbed by the dog's body. I am not saying this won't work, I am saying add fish oils also to the diet.

Black Cumin Seed
Black cumin is a part of the buttercup family and the seeds are dark, thin, and crescent-shaped when whole. The seeds have been used for many centuries in the Middle East, the Mediterranean and India. Today, black cumin seeds are used as a seasoning spice in different cuisines across the world due to their nutty flavor. Besides their culinary uses, black cumin seeds also have a wealth of important health benefits and are one of the most cherished medicinal seeds in history. The seeds of the black cumin plant contain over 100 chemical compounds, including some yet to be identified. In addition to what is believed to be the primary active ingredient, crystalline nigellone, black cumin seeds contain: thymoquinone, beta sitosterol, myristic acid, palmitic acid, palmitoleic acid, stearic acid, oleic acid, linoleic acid, arachidonic acid, protein, vitamin B1, vitamin B2, vitamin B3, folic acid, calcium, iron, copper, zinc, and phosphorous.
One recent study on black cumin seed oil demonstrated that it was effective against pancreatic cancer, one of the deadliest and most difficult to treat cancers.

NOTE: Those who decide to use black cumin seed oil should check labels and product information carefully. Black cumin is commonly referred to as black seed oil, black onion seed, black caraway, black sesame seed, and other names, but **only Nigella sativa is true black**

170

cumin. Black cumin seeds lower blood sugar levels and therefore should be consumed only after consulting with a vet/holistic vet. This has a VERY strong taste. Mix with something tasty your dog likes.

Dosage:
Small dogs: 1/2-1 teaspoon 2-3 times a day
Med/Large dogs: 1 teaspoon up to 1 TBSP 2-3 times a day
Give preferably on an empty stomach.

Noni Juice

Taking a daily dose of Noni Juice is as beneficial to pets as it is to humans. Adding Noni Juice to the food of dogs, cats and other animals has been shown to strengthen an animal's immune system. As pets age, they experience the same kinds of health problems as humans. In addition, the average pet diet is usually comprised of low quality ingredients. A low quality diet compromises a pet's immune system and lessens the ability to fight illness and disease.
Veterinarians who practice both traditional and holistic animal medicine recommend Noni Juice daily in the diet to assist in the treatment of viral infections, worms, digestive disorders, food allergies, recovery from surgery, and arthritis to name a few. There has been much success using Noni juice in treating pain, inflammation and ridding animals of worms. Using Noni juice eliminates the need for pharmaceutical muscle relaxants, anti-inflammatory and steroids. Noni juice enhances an animal's immune system, joint health, circulation, digestion, and various skin conditions.
Noni Juice can be added to the diet of dogs, cats, birds, hamsters, pet mice and larger animals such as horses and cows to strengthen and support the immune system, assist in cell regeneration, boost nutrient uptake, offer digestive support and increase energy. Safe for cats as well.

Dosage:
Up to 10 lbs: 5ml - 20ml per day
11-25 lbs: 20ml - 50ml per day
26-50 lbs: 50ml - 70ml per day
51 lbs and above: 70ml - 90ml per day

Giant Dogs: Start with between 20ml and 100ml per day and give an extra 15ml per 50 lbs.
The taste is strong.

ESSIAC TEA
(Ingredients in Essiac tea - Organic burdock root, organic sheep sorrel, organic (Turkey) rhubarb root and organic slippery elm bark.)

- Building immune system strength.
- Helping the body to destroy benign growths and tumors.
- Strengthening muscles, organs, and tissues.
- Removing toxic accumulation in the body, including heavy metals and other environmental toxins.
- Aiding in bowel detoxification and elimination.
- Adding strength and flexibility to bones, joints, and lungs.
- Blood purification.

As a general guide for treating animals, it is best to assess the dosage according to your pet's weight.
15 - 40lbs: 1/2 ounce of tea, twice per day
40 - 80lbs: 1 ounce of tea, twice per day
Over 80lbs: 2-3 ounces of tea, twice per day

WHO SHOULD **NOT** TAKE THE ESSIAC TEA:
If your dog has kidney disease, are prone to kidney stones, or kidney infections. The varying amounts of oxalic acids in this tea are irritating to the kidneys.

If your dog has ulcers or colitis.
The Essiac has an action of being a laxative or cathartic (depending on how much you take). Some properties in this root can be highly irritating to ulcers and colitis, exacerbating (or worsening) these conditions.
If your dog has tumors that are close to a major blood supply or an area of an organ that expansion of the tumor could have dire consequences.
In Rene's work, she reportedly noticed that in the beginning phase of a person taking this tea, the tumor could appear to enlarge before it

began to break down. (One of the reasons she was adamant that they take very small doses.) If you notice any sudden pain or unusual symptoms after beginning this tea, stop taking it. **Do not give to patients with a brain tumor.** This can be extremely detrimental in the brain tissue. Rapid or excess growth can put pressure on areas of the brain that affect body/mental function. If the tumor would break down, it can release pieces of the malignant tissue, which could cause a stroke. Circulation in the brain is unlike the rest of the body.

Astragalus *(Astragalus membranaceous)*
Immunostimulant, antiviral, anti-inflammatory, hypothyroid (mildly depresses thyroid function), hypotensive, digestive tonic. Works on immune systems, lungs, liver, heart, kidneys, thyroid, and digestive tract.
Astragalus is used for strengthening the body against viral infections of the respiratory and heart. Astragalus can be used for early treatment of a variety of respiratory infections, including kennel cough (Bordetella bronchiseptica). Astragalus helps to raise white blood cell counts and also boosts the body's immune system. Astragalus may be useful for helping the body protect itself and speed recovery from the damages of long term steroid medications. Astragalus is also useful in early stages of kidney infection and/or renal failure. Astragalus is non-toxic in any dosages.
Astragalus may help prevent the immunosuppression caused by chemotherapy agents. In addition, it has been found that Astragalus contains an alkaloid that inhibits the spread of melanoma, a skin cancer.

Panagamic Acid (B-15)
An ester derived from gluconic acid and dimethylglycine.
Based on research in humans, 125 mg – 2500 mg per day in divided doses is most commonly used. Although it can be taken with meals or on an empty stomach, it is most often advised to take between meals. It is best to divide the doses throughout the day. Panagamic Acid (B-15) is also found in the apricot kernels. For dogs you will need to half that dose and in smaller dogs even reduce it more. Human dosages are determined on a 150lb person. So adjust the dose for your dog by his weight.

Artemisinin
It is recommended that kidney and liver enzyme levels be monitored
though out your dog's treatment with Artemisinin. Artemisinin is an
extract isolated from the plant Artemisia annua, or sweet wormwood.
Artemisinin can kill iron-enriched breast cancer cells similar to the
way it kills malaria, making it a natural cancer treatment option for
breast cancer. Wormwood is used in natural heartworm treatments
and should be used with caution and under care of holistic vet. If your
dog is undergoing radiation you must **not** use this herbal. Works
against bone cancers and may work on brain cancers. Although
amounts are listed here, I recommend you giving this under the guidance of a holistic vet.

Dosage:
Small dogs (up to 30 lbs): 50mg twice a day
Medium dogs (over 30 lbs): 100mg twice a day
Large dogs (over 60 lbs): 150mg twice a day
Giant dogs (over 100 lbs): 200mg twice a day
Use this for two weeks on, then 4-5 days off, and then back to two
weeks. Repeat!

Bindweed extract
Bindweed extract has been shown to be helpful for numerous cancers,
including prostate cancer, lung cancer, liver cancers, and more. It is so
helpful, in fact, that it completely destroyed lethal cancer tumors in
laboratory mice.
Also called Convolvulaceae, bindweed extract is from the morning
glory family, which includes over 1600 species of plants. It is often
seen as a nuisance or a weed in many gardens but it is actually a very
effective cancer cure! Bindweed has also been used medicinally
for centuries as a natural laxative and for hypertension. In Chinese
Medicine it has been used as a salve for itching, pain and even tooth-
ache.

Medicinal Mushroom(s) especially Turkey Tail but a blend of mushrooms would work just as well. Yun Zhi is also known as *Coriolus
versicolor (Turkey Tail)*, *Trametes versicolor*, and *Polyporus
versicolor*. Most current cancer research in the United States refers to
it as *Trametes versicolor*. *Coriolus versicolor* is the most well-studied

medicinal mushroom in the world.

While there is not enough evidence to support using Turkey Tail alone for cancer treatment, there are mountains of evidence showing its efficacy as an adjuvant therapy. Particularly in cases of breast cancer, colorectal cancer, and gastric cancer, this mushroom therapy should be a component of the treatment plan, both during and after conventional treatments.

Mushrooms alleviate the side effects of chemotherapy. Promote vitality and stamina, inhibit pain and stimulate appetite. Mushrooms also stabilize the white blood cell count. White blood cells are the cells responsible for fighting infections and attacking tumor cells. Many integrative oncologists prescribe 3000-4500 mg (human dosage). Human dosing is based on a 150 lb person. Adjust accordingly to your dog's body weight.

More on mushrooms:
I believe taking Turkey Tail along with a mushroom combo would be great for the immune system and to help fight off the effects of chemo treatments if given. Great for building a strong immune system and fighting off radicals.

The Reishi mushroom has a strong taste to it.

Vitamin E Succinate (Dry E) (Recommended)
Each cell of the human body has a tiny furnace in it, known as the mitochondria, in which fuel (food) is burned to give energy to that cell. What vitamin E does is block that process in cancer cells. Without fuel, a cancerous cell soon dies of starvation no matter what stage it is in.

Some of these supplements may contain SOY! Avoid soy if at all possible. All soy contains GMOs. Look for this in a non-soy formula.

Bromelain
Taken from Washington State University...(pertains to people, not dog dosage. Dogs dosing is below) Bromelain is a water extract from pineapple stem that contains cysteine proteinases that have several therapeutic effects, including antimetastatic, antithrombotic, antiedematous, fibrolytic, and immunomodulatory actions.

Bromelain has been shown to inhibit growth of lung tumors in mice inoculated with tumor cells. Oral doses of Bromelain given in breast cancer patients for ten days enhanced monocyte cytotoxicity against breast cancer cells. Bromelain in doses of 3000mg have been found useful in preventing post surgical adhesions and is used, often in combination with other plant enzymes in the treatment of lymph edema. Reduce this amount for dogs (see below).

Because Bromelain has been shown to be generally safe in oral doses, integrative oncologists often use it for a variety of cancer-related conditions including post-radiotherapy fibrosis, post-surgical edema ileus, lymph edema, immunomodulation, and inflammatory bowel disorders.

Dosage:
Small dogs: 100mg - three times a day
Medium dogs: 200-300mg - three times a day
Large dogs: Up to 350mg - three times a day

L-Arginine (amino acid) and L-Glutamine
The basic reasons Arginine would be helpful for cancer patients is its ability to safely deliver more oxygen to oxygen-deprived tissues in the body. The entire world of alternative medicine agrees that getting more oxygen to the tissues is going to be bad news for any and all cancer cells because they have given up normal respiration for fermentation. When acid levels are high and oxygen levels are low we find cancer flourishing -a situation that orthodox oncology ignores. Arginine opens up the veins and arteries to increase blood flow and volume, thus increasing oxygen to the cells.

Quercetin
Human Dose is up to 1000 mg/day for up to 12 weeks have been shown well tolerated for human consumption. Quercetin is used in naturopathic medical practice in doses of 500-3000 mg/day as post-chemotherapy adjuvant therapy to stabilize the P53 gene. Since it inhibits the release of histamine it is also prescribed for cancer patients with Ig E-mediated allergies. Courses of Quercetin treatment may range from weeks to months.

Quercetin is an:

- Anti-allergenic
- Anti-carcinogenic
- Antifungal
- Anti-Inflammatory
- Anti-microbial
- Anti-viral

Used for allergies in place of Benadryl as well. Quercetin works for cancer but specifically these cancers for prevention and treatment.

- Breast cancer
- Colon cancer
- Endometrial cancer
- Ovarian cancer
- Prostate cancer

Use caution:
Very high doses can cause kidney damage. Do not give Quercetin to dog and cats with kidney disease. Quercetin can be administered for up to 12 consecutive weeks at a time. Only use Quercetin for as long as absolutely required. You should not keep your dog/cat permanently on Quercetin.

Dosage:
Small dogs: (Up to 20lbs) 50-160mg
Medium dogs: (20-50 lbs) 160-350mg
Large dogs: (50-100 lbs) 400-600mg

Rosehips
Dogs can greatly benefit from Rosehips as well. Rosehips is a great additional supplement for treating and preventing arthritis and many other diseases. It contains a high amount of vitamin C. It has a tart flavor but dogs don't seem to mind it. It's less expensive than Camu Camu. Camu Camu has one of the highest concentrations of vitamin C of any food source.

Dosage:
Small dogs: 1/4-1/2 teaspoon daily
Medium dogs: 1/2-1 teaspoon
Large dogs: 1-2 teaspoon

Unfiltered Raw Organic Apple Cider Vinegar ("Mother") (Recommended)
The body can be acidic and cancer grows in an acidic environment.
Add to daily meal if feeding wet foods. Add to cottage cheese or
yogurt or possibly water. Taken internally, ACV is credited with
maintaining the acid/alkaline balance of the digestive tract. To check
your dog's pH balance, pick up some pH strips at the drug store and
first thing in the morning test the dog's urine. If it reads anywhere
from 6.2 - 6.5, your dog's system is exactly where it should be. If your
dog has cancer, you need the pH level slightly higher than normal. If
it is 7.5 or higher, the diet you are feeding is too alkaline, and ACV
will re-establish the correct balance as well.

Dosage:
Small dogs (0-25 lbs): 1 teaspoon
Medium dogs (25-50 lbs): 1-2 teaspoons
Large dogs (50-80 lbs): 1 TBSP
Giant dogs (80+ lbs): 1 1/2-2 TBSP

Echinacea
Echinacea stimulates the white blood cells that help fight infections in
the body. Research has shown that Echinacea enhances the activity of
a particular type of white blood cells-macrophages. A particular
glycoprotein in Echinacea was found to significantly increase the killing
effect of macrophages on tumor cells. Echinacea benefits dogs by
boosting their immune system and helping their bodies fight bacteria,
viruses and other germs. Echinacea also has anti-inflammatory and
antimicrobial properties.

Colloidal Silver (Recommended)
This has many medicinal uses. It is a true antibiotic as well. It works
on cancers and helps build the immune system. Make sure you get
colloidal silver that is pure and of high quality. I recommend

Sovereign Silver brand. For fighting cancer, you can mix colloidal silver up to 50/50 with drinking water and then after a couple of weeks or so gradually back off from 2 tablespoons per day for small dogs up to 2 ounces per day for large dogs until the cancer is gone. Adding IP-6 along with colloidal silver makes this a powerful cancer fighter.

IP-6

IP-6 (inositol hexaphosphate) is a component of certain dietary fibers, particularly most cereal grains, legumes, and seeds high in oil. Many researchers believe that some of fiber's health benefits may be due to the antioxidant, immune enhancing, and cardiovascular supporting activities of IP-6. IP-6 has shown to have significant protective and growth regulating effects on various cells and tissues, including those of the colon, breast, and prostate. IP-6 has consistently demonstrated positive research results in animal and cell studies and has reported that IP-6 is effective in cancer prevention and control of tumor growth, progression, and metastasis. Its anticancer activity likely involves IP-6's immune stimulatory, potent antioxidant and anti-angiogenic effects. IP-6 has been shown to help treat kidney stones as well as high cholesterol and lipid levels.

Directions:
Powder-Mix 1 1/2 teaspoons (or up to 9 grams per day) with water. For systemic support, take on an empty stomach. For direct colon support, take just prior to or with meals.

Dosage:
Small dogs: 400 mg twice a day
Medium dogs: 800mg twice a day
Large dogs: 1200mg twice a day
Giant dogs: 1600 mg twice a day

Recent human studies of inositol for lung cancer showed that in a daily dose of 18 grams for 3 months, inositol was safe and well tolerated. IP-6 has anti-platelet activity, so it may increase the risk of bleeding when used with other anticoagulants or anti-platelet drugs. IP-6 can also bind with calcium, iron, magnesium, and zinc in the stomach and reduce their absorption.

Cell Stop (Recommended)
Nature has given us an army of cancer therapeutic substances from herbs, mushrooms, fruit and vegetable extracts that can help fight the very mechanisms cancers use to grow. Cell Stop is great for immune building as well as cancer killers. This contains Curcumin, Astragalus, Green Tea, a three mushroom blend, Quercetin, Broccoli Extract, Bitter Melon, Mangosteen fruit, Milk Thistle, Beta Glucan, Chamomile, Flaxseed, Pterostilbene and Se-Methylselenocysteine (Selenium). It contains these 17 powerful plant compounds that work together to target and disrupt abnormal cell growth on a cellular level. This is a great combination of ingredients all in one product. Whatever the dose is on the bottle, base it off of 150 lb person, then adjust for your dogs weight.

Selenium (Methylselenocysteine or Se-Methylselenocysteine)
Research notes show that breast cancer rates were low in areas where selenium levels in the soil and food were high. The same correlation was found between death rates and selenium levels. Similar correlations were subsequently found in animal studies. Methylselenocysteine does not accumulate in the body and is considered to be non-toxic.
In humans, it has been observed that a 200 mcg daily supplement given for four years led to a big reduction in cancer deaths and reduction in the incidence of prostate, lung, colorectal and some types of skin cancer. The symptoms of selenium deficiency include hypothyroidism, a weakened immune system and heart disease.

Dosage:
Small dogs: 10 mcg
Medium dogs: 25 mcg
Large dogs: 50 mcg

Colostrum
Colostrum from pasture-fed cows is much higher in immune factors than a human mother's colostrum! It's the immune boosting properties that make colostrum an important cancer fighting weapon.
Researchers have shown that colostrum is one of the most important nutritional supplements available for enhancing the immune system and helping in tissue repair. Colostrum works well for dogs and cats

with diarrhea and for weakened immune systems. Colostrum can be used in all animals and humans. Colostrum contains IgF (Epithelial growth Factors), IgF (Insulin-like Growth Factor), Transfer Factor, IgG (20 times that in human milk), PRP, etc. IGFs act as endocrine, autocrine and paracrine hormones enhancing cellular glucose uptake, and enhance synthesis of proteins, DNA, RNA and lipids. Without adequate EGFs, the body cannot repair damaged cells, no matter how good the patient is being fed.

Lactoferrin is another component of colostrum, which inhibits the growth of pathogenic organisms. Colostrum shows that it can be used to treat allergies, cancer, ulcerative colitis, diarrhea, poor wound healing, hepatitis C, bacterial and viral infections, multiple sclerosis, obesity and peptic ulcers. Colostrum is useful in the treatment of ulcerative colitis, inflammatory bowel disease and chemotherapy-induced mucositis. It's best to give at least 30 minutes before feeding time.

Dosage:
1/3 tsp per 25 pounds of body weight once per day.
You may notice changes as soon as one day to 2 months.

Pycnogenol (pine bark extract)
The dosage is 1 to 2 mg per pound of body weight per day.
With cancer, start out by doubling the dosage amount (for the first month) to give an initial boost to the free radical management in the patient's body before reducing back to the supplement dose.
Loaded with oligomeric proanthocyanidin compounds (OPCs). The same ingredient can be found in grape seeds.

DC-Y by MVP
I have to mention this one that I found recently through a friend. She has used this for herself, her horses and her dog. It's made for horses but the entire powder meal is nothing but anti-inflammatory herbs. The combination is awesome. The only thing it isn't organic. I wished it was but I still find that this product does such amazing things for cancer that I want to mention it. It's called DC-Y made by MVP and it's for horses. Cancer contains a lot of inflammation so this product combats that inflammation. It's very powerful and I do recommend this. If you want, you could purchase ingredients in it by buying or-

ganic powders and mixing them yourself. Make sure they are not sourced from China or India if you buy organic. You can find these on different sites like Starwest-Botanicals.com, Znaturalfoods.com, and MontainRoseHerbs.com. Make sure they are organic and from the USA preferably. Avoid China or India sources.

If I was to order organic powders, for the DC-Y closely related combo, I would buy: Devils Claw, Yucca, Grape Seed extract, Turmeric, White Willow Bark, and Boswellia/Frankincense. To add flavor you can use Rosehips, Camu Camu, Apple powder or Blueberry powder. Experiment with flavor that your dog will like. I found the organic apple powder at Znaturalfoods. Shop around these sites for the best prices and make you a good organic combo mix. That's my plan for me and my dogs as well.

DC-Y contains Devil's Claw, Yucca, Grape Seed Meal, Boswellia, Cat's Claw, Turmeric, Fever Few, and White Willow Bark...in that order. Also Alfalfa meal. It also contains natural and artificial flavors (apple).
There are many more supplements that work well in combination with others that I have not listed here.

Approximate dosing for dogs:
Small dogs: 1/4-1/2 tsp
Medium dogs: 1/2-1 tsp
Large dogs: 1 tsp -1 1/2 tsp
Giant dogs: 2 tsp

If you would like an organic version of anti-inflammatories, you can gather these ingredients online and purchase organic powders then combine. Choose Grape seed extract wisely. No skin or meat. Only seeds from grapes. Make sure it says 100% grape seed. Grape seed extract has terrific healing abilities for many diseases including cancer. You want to add flavor? You can find organic apple or blueberry powders as well.
I plan to buy organic powders and make my own. The costs will be close to the same and it will be organic. Well worth the money and allowing me to not worry about what's going in the body. If you want

organic powders and need help in finding them, just contact me through one of my websites and I will be glad to help you.

If your dog has leukemia, do not give since this contains Cat's Claw. If your dog has low blood pressure, Cat's Claw may lower blood pressure even more.

Because alfalfa has an estrogenic effect, patients with hormone-sensitive cancers should avoid alfalfa. You have hormone-sensitive cancer such as breast, prostate, cervical, or uterine cancers.

Shark Cartilage

I wouldn't normally recommend this because of the over killing of sharks but in the case of cancer, I will make an exception. There are some species of sharks not on the endangered list. So depends on manufacture on what sharks they are using as to whether I felt ok with it. Shark cartilage is expensive but consider the costs of modern treatments as opposed to safe alternatives. Initial studies showed in rats that when shark cartilage extract was injected into one eye along with a cancerous tumor and the other eye received only a cancerous tumor. After 19 days the eye that had injected both the tumor and the shark cartilage there was no tumor growth. In the eye with only the tumor, the tumor has grown much larger. So shark cartridge works at combating tumors by cutting off the blood supply. In these studies it shows that it doesn't have a direct effect on the tumor but yet cuts off the blood supply to the tumor therefore causing it to shrink. A good brand was mentioned and I found it at organicpharmacy.com. It's called Cartilade. It comes in capsules and powder. This is made for humans but if you are treating cancer for your dog, I would use human dosing, but work up to that amount. Another one is made for dogs and is called Wholistic Shark Cartilage.

Dosage:
Dogs Up to 30 lbs: 1/4 teaspoon
Dogs 31-60 lbs: 1/2 teaspoon
Dogs 61-90 lbs: 3/4 teaspoon
Dogs 91 lbs and over: 1 teaspoon

I would double this amount for treating cancer. It's also great for joints. For preventative/maintenance dosing, go with recommended dose on label.

Graviola (Soursop) Soursop contains folate, niacin, thiamin, vitamin C, calcium, magnesium, potassium, and fiber. This fruit is used to treat an upset stomach, coughs, asthma, skin conditions, gout, fever and as a mild, natural sedative. Graviola is considered an antioxidant and anti-inflammatory. Graviola has the ability to kill cancer cells specifically pancreatic cancer. A study that was conducted by the University of Nebraska Medical Center found that the extract can greatly reduce pancreatic cancer. Also used for treating bacterial infections. A really good brand is called **Amazon Thunder** at amazonthunder.com. It is organic and freeze dried.

Dosage:
Under 5 lbs: 1/4 capsule (or 4 or 5 drops for liquid types)
5 to 10 lbs: 1/2 capsule or 15 drops
30 to 50 lbs: 1 capsules or 25-30 drops
75 to 100 lbs: 1-2 capsules, 1/2 tsp or 2 droppers
Over 100 lbs: 2 capsules, 1/2 tsp or 2 droppers for every 100 lbs.

Start with low dose and work up to recommended dose

Other Options
Other options I would highly consider include intravenous vitamin C in high doses. This should be done by a holistic vet or Oncologist. Mistletoe -Two to three injections of Mistletoe per week are required to treat most cancers, and it is recommended that the injections be given in the morning. Can only be given by a Veterinarian.

K9-ACV Immunotherapy
There is a clinic called **Medivet Biologics** also found at medivetbiologics.com that offers a cancer vaccine. Not sure why it is called a vaccine. It's more like 3 injections given 4 weeks apart. They create the vaccine/injections using your own dog's cancer cells. Pricing for this is around $1,300. You can check it out as well. I found this slightly fascinating to say the least. (Medivet also offers Stem cell therapy). Medivet states it can treat these certain types of cancers:

- Lymphoma
- Mast cell tumor
- Sarcoma
- Osteosarcoma
- Melanoma
- Hemangiosarcoma (spleen or liver hemangiosarcoma cancer in dogs)
- Skin tumors
- mammary tumors
- Oral melanoma

Ideal Canine Cancer Patients

- Greater than 1 year of age
- Dogs with a solid cancerous tumor that is accessible for surgical removal
- Dogs must have a predicted survival greater than 1 month without therapy

The following list describes patients that are not suitable for the canine cancer treatment/vaccine.

- Leukemia or a cancerous tumor that cannot be removed
- Any previous forms of immunotherapy
- Pregnant dogs
- Histologic diagnosis of benign tumor in the resected tumor or low grade malignancy

This vaccine can be done by your own vet and it takes three injections given 4 weeks apart. Immunotherapy is a new ground-breaking treatment option for dogs with cancer. Many pet insurance companies offer coverage for the K9-ACV cancer treatment.

Hyperbaric Oxygen Chambers (Recommended)

Find a place that can do oxygen therapy for your pets. It would help to oxygenate the blood. This does not allow cancer cells to grow and travel throughout the system. Cancer cells cannot survive in an oxygenated body. So by increasing the oxygen in the blood, the cancer cells die. Same for starving it from having any sugar. I highly recommend looking into this. Find a facility in your area. Hyperbaric is used daily in cancer patients and has been extremely successful.

Magnetic Resonance
The **Magnesphere** is an FDA approved class 1 medical device that has been proven to lower stress and cortisol (the stress hormone) and restores the body to rest, repair and regenerate. This is relatively a new treatment and may be hard to access at this time. Go to YouTube to see this in action. Magnesphere has been shown to go from a dog dragging its hind legs to walking, a dog that had tumors and reducing and killing the tumor. This machine can do so much. Stress causes cancer. Yes even in our pets. Reducing stress heals the body as well.

Other things for your "To Do" list:
Get some sunshine: Soak up the rays. Just don't get burned and white dogs of course shouldn't stay out for more than 30 minutes or so in high heat since they burn much easier and faster. We all need sunshine.

Exercise
This is also **crucial** in cancer patients. Exercise helps reduce stress and providing oxygen to flow throughout the body. It's a healthy benefit for you and your dog. This will also heap your dog go into Ketosis much faster with the Ketogenic diet. You want to keep your dog lean when fighting cancer. A dog with joint issues, use Hydrotherapy.

Reduce stress: Make a calm quiet space for you and your dog. Stress can make cells grow. Play soft music, Meditate, Reiki, Acupuncture, and Yoga. Anything relaxing for you and your dog. If your dog seems stressed, you can add Ashwagandha to the diet daily. It helps for depression and anxiety. Also helps in fighting cancers.

 Do **not** use air fresheners in your home or anything with a fragrance. Buy top of the line (Merv 11 or 13 and above) air conditioning filters. Stay away from smog and exhaust from vehicles and busy highways. HEPA filters with carbon block or high Merv Ratings for your air filters. Check into HEPA air purifiers as well. Keep the air in your home clean and pure. Outside air is not clean and pure anymore.

Add an Essential oil diffuser to your home. Actually a couple of them around the house would be good. They come in different sizes. Add 3-5 drops of Frankincense and/or Myrrh for fighting cancer. Run this at night especially when you are sleeping in a closed bedroom. No cats allowed. Cats are very sensitive to essential oils. Use extreme caution.
Diffusers will cover only a certain amount of space just like your air purifiers. That's why it's good to have a couple of these in your house. I recommend a good organic essential oil.

Also, know that certain pet products - including the inflatable alternative to the so-called "cone of shame" are made of PVC, a known carcinogen. If my dog is battling cancer, PVC is the last substance I would strap around her neck! Try a neck pillow found in pet stores.

And overall, give love love love. Hug/kiss your pets. Give them massages. Show them lots of love and attention. Make them feel warm and fuzzy inside. It is the heart that can heal. Keep a positive attitude always and be happy, even during the most worrisome times. Make the moments count!

If your pet experiences unusual side effects, substitute with something else. Adverse reactions to the herbs recommended are unusual. But just like people, allergic reactions are possible. Do not give your dog softgels. They will not dissolve.

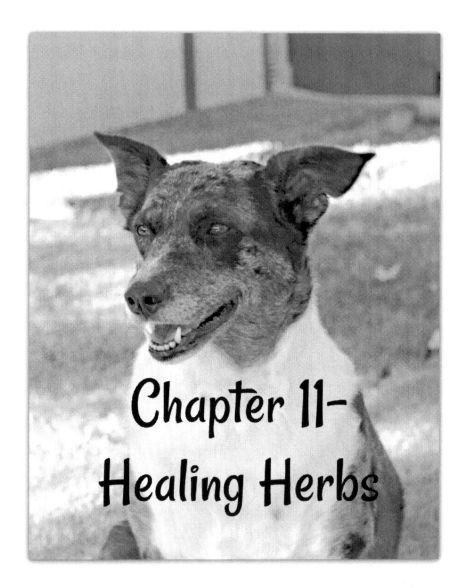

Chapter 11–
Healing Herbs

Chapter 11
Healing Herbs

This information was gathered from multiple sources and created for you to learn about these herbs.

Astragalus *(Astragalus membranaceous)*
Immunostimulant, antiviral, anti-inflammatory, hypothyroid (mildly

depresses thyroid function), hypotensive, digestive tonic. Works on immune systems, lungs, liver, heart, kidneys, thyroid, and digestive tract.

Astragalus is used for strengthening the body against viral infections of the respiratory and heart. Astragalus can be used for early treatment of a variety of respiratory infections, including kennel cough (Bordetella bronchiseptica). Astragalus helps to raise white blood cell counts and also boosts the body's immune system. Astragalus may be useful for helping the body protect itself and speed recovery from the damages of long term steroid medications. Astragalus is also useful in early stages of kidney infection and/or renal failure. Astragalus is non-toxic in any dosages.

Moringa
Moringa contains 46 antioxidants, 90 nutrients including calcium, trace minerals, iron, and all 9 essential amino acids.
Moringa also contains powerful antioxidants, and has anti-fungal, antibacterial and anti-inflammatory properties. A very powerful green food.

Dosage:
Small dogs/cats (up to 20 lbs): 1/4 - 1/2 teaspoon
Medium dogs (20-50 lbs): 1 teaspoon
Large dogs (50-100 lbs): 1 1/2-2 teaspoons
Giant dogs (100+ lbs): 1 tablespoon

This is just a general guideline and can be adjusted as needed.

Mullein
Mullein soothes and protects mucous membranes. It is an expectorant and can suppress cough (kennel cough) and treating asthma. Works with flu, coughs etc.

The flowers, in the form of an oil infusion, also have antimicrobial properties and are effective in treating ear infections, including those caused by ear mites. The flower oil infusion can also be used to fight against fleas and mange.

Milk Thistle
Milk thistle is well known as an **herb for the liver** both for humans and pets. Milk thistle contains a flavonoid called silymarin. Extensive research has found that silymarin is safe and effective in treating a variety of liver diseases and other conditions, from kidney disease to mushroom or lead poisoning. It works by removing toxins trying to bind to the liver and by causing the liver to regenerate more quickly.

Works on:

- Chronic inflammatory liver disorders
- Liver tumors
- Leptospirosis
- Pancreatitis
- Fatty liver

Milk thistle is not effective in treating advanced liver cirrhosis.
Milk thistle is very safe on dogs. If milk thistle causes upset stomach, gas, or mild diarrhea in your dogs, simply reduce the dosage. Milk thistle should **not** be given to healthy dogs as a daily supplement. Some studies show that long-term use of very high dosages of milk thistle will eventually suppress liver function.

Given for up to three months for detox or removing toxins should be long enough.

Rosehips
Rosehips have been known for its ability to reduce the symptoms of rheumatoid arthritis, some respiratory conditions, prevent cancer, lower cholesterol, manage diabetes and boost the immune system. The vitamins and minerals included in rosehips is vitamin C, A, E, and B-complex, as well as calcium, iron, selenium, manganese, magnesium, phosphorous, potassium, sulfur, silicon, and zinc.

The amount of antioxidants in rose hips is particularly useful in keeping the body healthy.

Rosehips has an impressive amount of vitamin C, which is one of the best methods to boost the immune system. Vitamin C stimulates white blood cells and is also essential in the prevention of asthma and the general health of the respiratory system. This also can be seen in the reduction of respiratory conditions such as colds and flu's through the intake of Rosehips and its high levels of vitamin C.

Rosehips can regulate the blood sugar levels of the body for anyone suffering from diabetes. By keeping the balance of insulin and glucose in the body, Rosehips can prevent fluctuations in blood sugar. Rosehips is also used as a diuretic which can help eliminate toxins from the body. Rosehips contain a good amount of iron which can help prevent anemia and also keep your organs well oxygenated. Collagen, along with the other minerals in Rosehips, can help prevent Osteoporosis. Safe for cats as well.

Dosage:
Small dogs: 1/4-1/2 teaspoon daily
Medium dogs: 1/2-1 teaspoon
Large dogs: 1-2 teaspoon

Slippery Elm (Ulmus fulva)
Slippery Elm is very safe and non-toxic. It can be used both internally and externally. Slippery Elm is one of the herbs used in Essiac Tea.

In the gastrointestinal tract, Slippery Elm acts directly. It resembles a natural "Pepto-Bismol." (Pepto-Bismol itself should not be used because it contains salicylate, a.k.a. aspirin).
Slippery Elm coats, soothes, and lubricates the mucus membranes lining of the digestive tract. Slippery Elm is an excellent treatment for ulcers, gastritis, colitis, and other inflammatory bowel problems. It is high in fiber, and so helps normalize intestinal action. It can also be used to relieve diarrhea and constipation. It also may help with nausea and vomiting.
Slippery Elm contains many nutrients beneficial for recuperating pets, and it may stay down when other foods are not tolerated. Slippery Elm may interfere with the absorption of certain minerals and pharmaceuticals, so is best given separately from any medications.

Give a dose before or with meals for digestive tract problems, such as

191

inflammatory bowel disease, until symptoms resolve.

Slippery Elm also has a calming effect creating a more relaxed sleep.

Turmeric
Turmeric is becoming very popular as a cure for cancers.
Turmeric (Curcumin) has extreme anti-cancer properties. It has proven to cure some cancers because it inhibits growth of tumors, shrinks existing ones and prevents new tumors from developing.

Turmeric has been found to be a good pain reliever to dogs. No turmeric side effects to worry about, even if a large dose is given. It's a great herb to add to the dog's food if it suffers from arthritis. An animal that's had a skin injury can be helped by turmeric's antibiotic and anti-inflammatory properties.

To treat a skin issue, simply mix honey with turmeric to form a paste and apply it to the abrasion.

Has been known to work on:

- Blocking inflammation
- Killing bacteria
- Improves health of the heart
- Antioxidant, carcinogenic, antibiotic, anti-inflammatory
- Stomach ailments
- Kills parasites
- Heals damage done from long-term diabetes

The dose for pain in dogs is 1/8 to 1/4 tsp. for every 10 pounds of dog's weight.

Turmeric should not to be given to dogs prone to kidney stones. Turmeric isn't supposed to be given with blood thinners. Turmeric should not be combined with drugs that reduce stomach acid (Pepsid, Zantac etc), as the body will actually increase its production of stomach acid, and thus, lead to nausea, stomach pain, bloating, and esophagus damage.

Burdock Root
Burdock Root is a blood-purifying, hair-regrowing and cancer-fighting herb.

Its uses:

- Antioxidant
- Blood cleansing
- Liver and gallbladder stimulant
- Diuretic

Burdock is an effective herb for the detoxification of the body. It can remove toxic substances that are threatening the health of our dogs. Use it regularly as a preventative, especially if you have a breed of dog that's prone to cancer(such as a Boxer). Burdock can be used as a long-term liver tonic to clean and build the blood.

It is also useful in the treatment of arthritis, cancer, rheumatoid disorders, and kidney and bladder diseases. It also has been used as a diuretic that helps to eliminate waste materials from the body.

Chamomile
Used for anxiety, and nervous disorders, skin inflammation, flatulence and indigestion. One of the best known and most widely used plants in the world, chamomile is gentle, can be used internally and externally in teas, tinctures, salves, compresses and rinses. Helps to calm and relax the dog or person. Chamomile should not be given to cats.

Dandelion (Taraxacum officinale)
Dandelion has been used for digestive and liver (root); Pancreatitis, edema (leaf), Anemia, Kidney/Bladder.

The leaf and root are good for many conditions involving edema (water retention) and the flowers are high in antioxidants. You can use root and leaf together and most of all for liver, kidney and heart disease in dogs.

Dandelion should not be used in cases of bile duct obstruction or acute gallbladder inflammation. The high mineral content may affect the absorption of a certain class of antibiotics (quinolones).

Dandelion leaf is particularly useful in animals that have a chronic problem with indigestion. If your dog has frequent gas and/or passes food that does not appear digested, apply a few drops of dandelion tincture on his/her tongue.

Dandelion is popular and is a safe but powerful diuretic and liver stimulant. Dandelion works with congestive heart failure, pulmonary edema, arthritis, gallbladder disease and kidney stones. Drugs such as Lasix are often used to drain off excess fluid from the body and help the elimination of waste. Pharmaceutical diuretics are fast-acting and very effective, but while they do a good job at reducing fluid buildup, they tend not to discriminate between what the body needs to keep and what it needs to lose. The body often loses too much potassium, a crucial heart and brain chemical, through urination. In this event, potassium must be supplemented throughout the therapy. Dandelion leaf on the other hand, contains its own rich source of potassium that the body can absorb.
While dandelion leaves are used as a diuretic, the root holds its own usefulness as a safe liver tonic. The liver is the primary filtering organ and responsible for removing toxins from the blood for elimination in the kidneys. And while dandelion leaf tea or tincture may do much toward relieving the symptoms through a nutritive/diuretic action, the root will work closer to the underlying causes.

Dandelion does not further irritate an already inflamed condition. Dandelion was shown to be effective in treating inflammatory diseases of the liver and the gall bladder including gallstones.

Devil's Claw
Used for reducing inflammation, especially with Osteoarthritis. There is a great range of dose with Devil's Claw. It's best to start with small amount and work up. Side effects if giving too much can include diarrhea as with all herbs and supplements although not common. Devil's Claw is used as an anti-inflammatory for arthritis. Devil's Claw is used for all types of muscle pain, and some forms of

digestive upset – although it should not be used with ulcers. It helps your dog feel better without NSAIDs. This works well and it's safe. Devil's Claw has been used to treat loss of appetite, rheumatism, arthritis, fever, tendonitis, gastrointestinal problems, and liver and gallbladder problems. Devil's Claw is also used as a pain reliever (analgesic), sedative, and diuretic.

Dosage:
Small dogs: 250 mg
Medium/Large dogs: 500 mg
Giant dogs: Up to 1000 mg

Echinacea
Echinacea has long been used for infections and as a blood purifier. Echinacea stimulates the immune system to help fight viral and bacterial infections. Echinacea is an immune stimulant that helps the body defend itself against viral infection more effectively.
Because of its powerful immune boosting ability, its best to only take Echinacea for a short period of time, usually from a few days to a few weeks, depending on your illness. This short period will activate your immune system.

Essiac Tea
Essiac may help your pet's health by:
- Building immune system
- Helping the body to destroy benign growths and tumors.
- Strengthening soft tissues.
- Removing toxins from the body, including heavy metals and other environmental toxins.
- Digestive System

Dosage:
15 to 40lbs: 1/2 ounce of tea, twice per day
40 - 80lbs: 1 ounce of tea, twice per day
Over 80lbs: 2-3 ounces of tea, twice per day
Give one hour before or two hours after a meal whenever possible.
Best method - syringe, eyedropper, food dish, etc.
You can mix with broth or with water or mix with food.

You should bear in mind that giving your pet Essiac tea will make them thirsty, so make sure they have plenty of water available. Drinking more water will help flush the system.

Watch out for diarrhea when giving your pet Essiac, if it is excessive; stop giving your pet Essiac until stools are back to normal, and then start back on a smaller dosage.

The best results are seen in animals that had a much larger dose than these recommended doses. Rhubarb is a laxative, and that is probably the main reason it is needed in Essiac. Dogs have much shorter digestive systems than people, and they are much more susceptible to diarrhea. The best way to decide what the dose for a pet should be is to increase the amount until they get diarrhea and then back off.

WHO SHOULD NOT TAKE THE ESSIAC TEA: If your dog has kidney disease, are prone to kidney stones, or kidney infections. The varying amounts of oxalic acids in this tea are irritating to the kidneys. If your dog has ulcers or GI Tract issues, do not give. Some properties in this root can be irritating to ulcers and colitis making these conditions worse.

If your dog has tumors that are close to a major blood supply or an area of an organ that expansion of the tumor could have dire consequences. **Do not give to patients with a brain tumor.** This can be extremely detrimental in the brain tissue. Rapid or excess growth can put pressure on areas of the brain that affect body/mental function.

Ginger Root
Ginger may be one of the most important plants used in herbal medicine. Ginger is one of the most prescribed herbs and is used in the treatment of colds for its ability to eliminate toxins and raise body heat.

Ginger Side Effects: Ginger is a blood thinner, if you are taking prescription blood thinners, have a bleeding disorder, or have gallbladder disease don't take medicinal doses of ginger.
Ginger can be used safely to treat a wide range of health problems,

from simple nausea to arthritis. Ginger combines well with many herbs, improving taste and potency.

Avoid Ginger from countries such as China and India. That includes organic as well.

Amla

Amla fruit (Emblica officinalis), also known as Indian Gooseberry or Amalaki, is one of the richest sources of bioflavonoids and vitamin C. This plum-sized fruit is admired for its anti-aging and immune system-enhancing properties. Each Amla fruit contains up to 700 mg of vitamin C.

It has been used for anemia, asthma, bleeding gums, diabetes, colds, chronic lung disease, hypertension, yeast infections, and cancer. It also increases lean body mass, accelerates the repair and regeneration of connective tissue, and enhances interferon and corticosteroid production.

Amla also acts as an antacid and anti-tumorigenic agent. In addition, it increases protein synthesis and is useful in cases of hypoglycemia. Amla powder is also rich in fiber, which helps support digestion and prevents constipation. Amla may also help reduce acidity in the gut, protect from gallbladder infections, treat diabetes, and reduce the risk for gastrointestinal cancer and cancer of the respiratory tract.

Dosage:
Small dogs: 500mg
Medium dogs: 750mg
Large dogs: 1000 mg

Hawthorn

Hawthorn helps prevent and treat congestive heart failure in senior dogs (and people), and tones the hearts of younger dogs who have survived heartworm disease. Older dogs, especially those with cardiac or renal problems, can benefit from Hawthorn.

Unlike most medications, tonic herbs do not suppress or replace natural functions in the body. Instead, they naturally help improve the body as a whole. Most tonic herbs do their work by providing special nutrients, enzymes that the body needs to bring overstressed organs and systems into functioning more appropriately. Hawthorn works over a period of time with daily use and improves the heart. Hawthorn helps support the heart in ways that no food or drug can. Hawthorn helps to increase circulation and the transport of nutrients and oxygen throughout the body. Hawthorn has the ability to strengthen a weak or erratic heartbeat – such as that of elderly or energetically challenged dogs. Hawthorn is very, very safe. In the hundreds of animal studies that have been conducted with this herb in the last 100 years, Hawthorn has shown extremely low toxicity in every animal tested.

Hawthorn is useful in the daily care of any older dog, but especially those who suffer from chronic heart problems and that have a weakened heart to be able to help it to pump blood. Hawthorn is also useful in cases of renal failure, especially in early stages. When combined with Ginkgo Biloba, Hawthorn may be useful for getting more blood and oxygen into renal arteries and smaller vessels of the kidneys.

Boswellia
Boswellia has also been shown in preliminary research to be effective at reducing swelling around brain tumors.
A study performed in 2004 shows that Boswellia is an herb that lives up to its reputation. Twenty Four dogs with chronic joint pain were administered a dose of Boswellia once a week for 6 weeks. After just a couple weeks 71 percent of the dogs showed improvement. The research showed that improvement was gradual but Boswellia did seem to help reduce local pain and stiff gaits. Boswellia is one herb that seems to work well.

Camu Camu (Myrciaria dubia)
Camu Camu is high in vitamin C and has been shown to reduce inflammation, detoxify the body, and prevent viral infections.

Camu Camu contains a huge amount of vitamin C. Camu Camu has one of the highest concentrations of vitamin C of any food source.
Camu Camu has been known to prevent certain cognitive disorders, such as Alzheimer's disease and dementia. It can also boost cognitive ability in younger people, increasing focus, memory, and concentration skills.
Camu Camu is not known as an allergenic food, and can be taken in

conjunction with other pharmaceuticals and supplements.

Hydrangea Root
A flower essence helps to naturally dissolve kidney stones and struvite crystals. A safe, natural alternative treatment. Used for kidney support, as a diuretic, eliminates swelling and fluid retention and increases the flow of urine. Will dissolve/remove bladder/struvite and kidney stones and relieve the pain they cause, and alleviate backache due to kidney issues. Hydrangea Root has been used to treat chronic rheumatoid arthritis and the swelling of arthritis (by reducing calcium deposits), gout and edema.

Hydrangea Root has also been used to help dissolve bone spurs or calcification of muscles. It appears to help the body put calcium back into in the system.
Hydrangea Root has an anti-inflammatory action that have a cortisone-like effect. This is useful for kidney infection and inflammation as well as for arthritis. It has also been used to break up lumps and tumors. It increases the production of urine (a diuretic) and also has a mild laxative effect. It may be combined with other herbs like marshmallow. Specific breeds at highest risk for kidney and bladder stones include Miniature Schnauzers, Shih Tzu's, the Bichon Frise, Cocker Spaniels and Lhasa Apso's. Keep PH levels between 6-7 but no higher than 7. I recommend closer to the 7PH mark for cancer patients.

Hydrangea Root Capsule Dosage:
Kidney stones: Give for 6-8 weeks, then re-test
Struvite crystals: Give for 6 weeks, then re-test
Oxalate stones: Surgery may be required.

Dosage:
up to 25lbs: 1/2 capsule with food 3 times a day
25-50 lbs: 1 capsule with food 3 times a day
50-75lbs: 1 1/2 capsules with food 3 times a day
75lbs+: 2 capsules with food 3 times a day

Warning: Certain parts of hydrangeas are particularly dangerous and toxic to dogs. These parts are the buds and the leaves. Owners *of dogs should make sure that their pets steer clear of hydrangeas, and make sure that the buds and leaves go nowhere near their mouths. Hydrangea <u>Root</u> is safe!*

Ashwagandha
Ashwagandha has been used to promote health and longevity. Ashwagandha is admired for its anti-aging properties. It is used to enhance the immune system and treat anemia, inflammation, bacterial infection, and diarrhea. It is also thought to improve the quality of bodily tissues. Its herbal actions span a wide range from adaptogenic to sedative.

 Ashwagandha helps relieve general aches and pains. Ashwagandha is an excellent hematinic and contains high levels of iron and free amino acids such as glycine, valine, tyrosine, proline, and alanine. This herb has been shown to be safe for long-term use. Ashwagandha has anti-inflammatory, diuretic, sedative, antibacterial, and anti-fungal activity. It also has anti-tumorigenic uses in animals.

Ashwagandha is used for anxiety and depression and helps relieve stress. Supports a healthy nervous system.

Dosage: (up to twice a day)
Small dogs: 500mg
Medium dogs: 1,000mg
Large dogs: 1,500mg

Astragalus *(Astragalus membranaceous)*
Immunostimulant, antiviral, anti-inflammatory, hypothyroid (mildly depresses thyroid function), hypotensive, digestive tonic. Works on immune systems, lungs, liver, heart, kidneys, thyroid, and digestive tract.

Astragalus is used for strengthening the body against viral infections of the respiratory and heart. Astragalus can be used for early treatment of a variety of respiratory infections, including kennel cough (Bordetella bronchiseptica). Astragalus helps to raise white blood cell counts and also boosts the body's immune system. Astragalus may be useful for helping the body protect itself and speed recovery from the damages of long term steroid medications. Astragalus is also useful in early stages of kidney infection and/or renal failure. Astragalus is non-toxic in any dosages.

Astragalus may help prevent the immunosuppression caused by chemotherapy agents. In addition, it has been found that Astragalus contains an alkaloid that inhibits the spread of melanoma, a skin cancer.

Quercetin

Flavonoids, such as Quercetin, are antioxidants. They scavenge particles in the body known as free radicals which damage cell membranes and cause cell death. They may reduce or even help prevent some of the damage free radicals cause.

Quercetin prevents immune cells from releasing histamines, which are chemicals that cause allergic reactions. As a result, Quercetin may help reduce symptoms of allergies, including runny nose, watery eyes, hives, and swelling of the face and lips.

Scientists have considered Quercetin, and other flavonoids contained in fruits and vegetables, important in cancer prevention. People who eat more fruits and vegetables tend to have lower risk of certain types of cancer. Flavonoids have anti-cancer properties. Quercetin and other flavonoids have been shown in these studies to inhibit the growth of cancer cells from breast, colon, prostate, ovarian, endometrial, and lung tumors. A frequent intake of Quercetin-rich foods was associated with lower lung cancer risk.

Quercetin supplements are available as pills or capsules. They are often packaged with Bromelain (an enzyme found in pineapple) because both are anti-inflammatories.

Chlorella

Chlorella is blue - green algae like its cousin spirulina. Chlorella's rich green color comes from a high concentration of chlorophyll. Chlorella contains whole range of B vitamins, vitamin C and E, amino acids and trace minerals. It contains more vitamin B-12 than liver. Chlorella is a great supplement to help boost the immune system and to help the body detoxify as well from heavy metals. Helps in fighting cancer by building the immune system. Also lowers blood sugars and cholesterol.

Different combinations of herbs and supplements specific for illness/disease. Give at least 3-5 of each mixed. Buy organic if at all possible.

Herbs and supplements great for kidney and urinary support including struvite stones:
Uva Ursi
Hydrangea Root
Marshmallow Root
Goldenrod
Chanca Piedra (stone breaker)
Organic Dandelion
Apple Cider Vinegar (raw, unfiltered)
Horsetail (use with caution when using other herbs)
Plantain (use with caution)
Olive Leaf
Organic Mushrooms
Humic/Fulvic Acid
Organic Alfalfa
IP-6
Pumpkin Seeds
Cranberry
L-Histidine (amino acid)
N-acetylcysteine (NAC)
Vitamin C (Magnesium Ascorbate)
Magnesium Citrate

Anti-inflammatory Herbs
(Great for any type of infection in the body, joint issues as well as cancer.)
Devil's Claw
Cat's Claw
Boswellia
Turmeric
Yucca root
Fever Few
White Willow Bark
Grape Seed Extract (Seeds Only)
Ginger

Organic Alfalfa

Kennel cough or cough, flu, sneezing, runny nose:
Fenugreek
Mullein
Vitamin C (Magnesium Ascorbate) to bowel tolerance
Organic Astragalus
Echinacea
Organic Mushrooms
Grape Seed Extract (organic)
Diffuse the essential oils lavender and eucalyptus.
N-acetylcysteine (amino acid)
Licorice and Deglycrrhizinated Licorice (DGL) (small amounts
and/or short term use) (Do not use with heart disease)

Thyroid support:
Licorice and Deglycrrhizinated Licorice (DGL) (small amounts
and/or short term use) (Do not use with heart disease)
Organic Astragalus
Siberian Ginseng (also known as Eleuthero Root)
Bladderwrack
Organic Ashwagandha Root
Gotu Kola (Can be toxic in large doses)

Diabetes support:
Grape Seed Extract (organic)
Fenugreek
Gymnema Sylvestre
Turmeric
Golden Seal

Natural deworming (not including heartworm):
Diatomaceous Earth (may not kill tapeworms)
Organic Raw Pumpkin Seeds/Powder

There are herbs you can use but will need to be used under the care of
a holistic vet so I won't mention them here. These mentioned above
are safe.

Seizures:
Organic Cannabis Oil (CBD) (no seeds)
Passion Flower
Valerian
Chamomile
Blue Vervain
Skullcap

Candida/Yeast:
Pau D'Arco
Golden Seal (do not give to puppies)
Garlic
Oregano Oil (short term use)
Apple Cider Vinegar (raw, unfiltered)
Probiotics/Digestive Enzymes
Organic Coconut Oil
Grapefruit Seed Extract
Olive Leaf
Saccharomyces boulardii (found in some probiotics)

Depression/Moodiness/Stress:
Siberian Ginseng (also known as Eleuthero Root)
Organic Ashwagandha
Organic Cannabis Oil (CBD)
Bacopa
SAMe (S-adenosylmethionine)
Gamma-amino butyric acid (GABA)

Dementia/Cognitive Dysfunction:
Bacopa
MCT Oil/Coconut oil (reports that coconut oil has reversed the process)
Ginkgo Biloba
Gotu Kola
Organic Cannabis Oil (CBD)
Organic Turmeric
Fish oils
SAMe (S-adenosylmethionine)
7-HMRlignans from Norwegian Spruce Tree (Swanson sells it)

Hormone balancer:
Dong Quai (Angelica sinensis)
Diindolylmethane (DIM) 10mg (crucifers like broccoli, cauliflower etc)
7-HMRlignans from Norwegian Spruce Tree (Swanson sells it)
DHEA (10-25mg)
SAMe (S-adenosylmethionine)
Wild Yam

Leaky Gut/ GI Tract Issues/Allergies/Ulcers
Slippery Elm
L-Glutamine
Colostrum
Probiotics
Digestive Enzymes (higher doses)
L-Histidine (amino acid)
N-acetylcysteine (amino acid) *(also used for Tylenol toxicity)*
Bee Pollen
Licorice and Deglycrrhizinated Licorice (DGL) (small amounts or short term use) (Do not use with heart disease)
Cat's Claw
Oregon Grape

Pancreas/Pancreatitis
Cat's Claw
Digestive Enzymes (High in amylase, Lipase, pancreas, ox bile etc)
Probiotics (start 2 billion and work up)
Colostrum
Nigella sativa
Gamma-amino butyric acid (GABA)
Fenugreek
Raw Pancreas
Ancestral Grass Fed Beef Pancreas supplement

If dosage isn't listed under each supplement, use this chart for dosing:

Herb Dosage

Weight	Tincture	0 Capsule	Tea	Powder
5-10 lbs	2 drops	1/2 cap	1 tsp	1/4 tsp
10-20 lbs	4 drops	1 cap	2 tsp	1/4-1/2 tsp
20-30 lbs	6 drops	1 cap	1 TBSP	1/2 tsp
30-50 lbs	6 drops	2 caps	4 tsp	1/2-1 tsp
50-70 lbs	6-10 drops	2 caps	5 tsp	1 tsp
70-90 lbs	14-18 drops	3 caps	2 TBSP	1 1/2 tsp
90-110 lbs	18-22 drops	4 caps	3 TBSP	2 tsp
110-150 lbs	22-26 drops	4 caps	4 TBSP	2 1/2 tsp
150-180 lbs	26-30 drops	5 caps	5 TBSP	3 tsp

All herbs should be given 5 days on and 2 days off. The body needs a break to catch up.

If your pet experiences unusual side effects, substitute with something else. Adverse reactions to the herbs recommended are unusual. But just like people, allergic reactions are possible. Do not give your dog softgels. They do not dissolve.

Some herbs can be toxic in higher doses and should be used under a holistic vet's supervision. The ones listed here are safe unless a note with it says otherwise.

For finding the best quality herbs out there, check out the Health Rangers (Mike Adams) products. A little pricey but I totally trust his products as they have all been tested in his lab for purity and none will ever come from China. Also products at organixx.com. Always buy organic for full benefits. These are human supplements so check the ingredients to make sure they are safe for dogs. Grapes are in some of the products. Grape seeds only are safe.

Avoid Turmeric, Ginger and Garlic from countries such as China and India. That includes organic as well.

If your dog has any type of kidney or liver disease or chronic illness, please check with your vet before giving any type of herbal supplements.

Extra tips for using Colloidal Silver

- Spray hot spots, scrapes, cuts, burns, and infections to help heal
- Put into ear for earaches, ear mites, and yeasty ears.
- Helps with Cystitis and UTI's
- Add drops in eyes to help with pink eye, dry eyes, sty's, and other eye infections. (half distilled water and half CS)
- Brush teeth to prevent decay and bad breath (also spray in mouth daily)
- Spray in mouth on gums and teeth to help keep down tarter build up
- Reduces symptoms of flu, cold, respiratory
- Add to organic chemical-free shampoo to become a disinfectant
- Spray water bowl before filling with filtered water to help prevent mold and bacteria (purifies water also)

Recommended Dosing

Up to 10lbs	1 tsp
11-25lbs	1 1/3 tsp
26-40lbs	2 tsp
41-55lbs	2 1/2 tsp
56-80lbs	3 tsp
81-100lbs	3 1/2 tsp
101-150lbs	4 tsp
151-200+lbs	4-5 tsp

Find us at:
www.HolisticAndOrganixPetShoppe.com
www.CanineArthritisAndJoint.com

Disclaimer: The information herein is intended for informational, educational purposes only and is not a substitute for medical advice, diagnosis or treatment. Do not attempt to self-diagnose or treat any health condition. You should always consult with a healthcare professional before starting any diet, exercise or supplementation program, before taking any medication, or if you have or suspect your pet may have a health problem. The Food and Drug Administration has not evaluated the information contained herein. The information presented here is not meant to replace your vets advice or prescribed medications, but only to suggest additional options to explore, based on your dog's health condition.

Limit of Liability/Disclaimer of Warranty: While the author has used her best efforts in preparing this book, she makes no representations or warranties with respect to the accuracy or completeness of the contents of this book. You should consult with a professional when appropriate. Author & publisher will not be liable for any loss of profit or any other commercial damages, including but not limited to special, incidental, consequential, or other damages.

Copyright © Debbie Daniel
978-1978332942
Revised Edition October 23rd, 2017
All rights reserved. No part of this book may be reproduced, scanned, or distributed in any printed or electronic form without permission.

Printed in the United States of America
Cover designed by Debbie Daniel

Notes about the conventional veterinarian profession:

You may find in this book that I am pretty hard on veterinarians. And the reason is because they are our "go to" source. The middle man between Big Pharma, pet foods and our pets. I feel that a good veterinarian is hard to find. Many are in a hurry, are all about the money or don't care enough to listen or help your pets. I hope veterinarians will wake up to the fact that this isn't acceptable and us pet parents are starting to stand up for our pets and demand better care that isn't guided by pharmaceutical companies and pet food companies or greed. So find a good vet that understands your needs and desires for your pets. And holistic vets may not be completely holistic. Learn the differences. Do they recommend optional vaccines?

I understand vets may not always know about nutrition nor do they quite understand raw diets due to the talk traveling throughout the vet profession to advise against raw diets. But I hope that veterinarians in the future will have the desire to look outside these conventional means and learn how to integrate alternative methods as well. We need to keep the body healthy instead of waiting to treat a sick body. Vets can recommend wellness exams instead of pushing vaccines for income purposes. We all need to eat but it is their oath of the profession to provide medical care to pets even while healthy and NOT push unhealthy medications and vaccines on pets for income purposes. Vets are crucial in emergencies and extreme illnesses but mild illness (such as allergies etc) or wellness exams should not consist of vaccines or risky medications and garbage prescription pet foods. Veterinarians are not nutritionists and most vet nutritionists work for pet food companies. So it is crucial that vets support and learn about homemade diets. This is our future.

A wellness exam can/should consist of yearly blood work (CBC), urinalysis, thyroid check, heartworm check, heart check, teeth inspection/cleaning if needed, x-rays if needed, as well as recommending joint supplements for all ages. An overall health wellness exam to help your pet live longer. Therefore vets will have a client for life. A wellness exam can be a lot of money coming in if they will recommend this instead of vaccines to get you in the door. This is a win-win situation.

21110828R00117

Made in the USA
San Bernardino, CA
01 January 2019